Banking Beyond Borders Learnings from a Veteran Banker

Mohan Vasant Tanksale

Printed in India

IndiePress

ISBN: 978-93-6045-660-3

First Printing, 2024

IndiePress

A division of Nasadiya Technologies Private Ltd.

Koramangala, Bangalore

Karnataka-560029

http://indiepress.in/

Edited by Rechal Fernandes

Typeset by Rechal Fernandes

Book Cover designed by Malik

Publishing Consultant – Rechal Fernandes

This book is dedicated to
Buddhidevata Shri Ganesha,
our parents and the Indian Banking industry

Contents

Acknowledgements

A book is never complete without its acknowledgements and life is never complete without gratitude and blessings.

To begin with I must show thankfulness and gratitude to my parents, who lived honest, upright lives steeped in moral and spiritual values. I believe my conditioning and their blessings are the biggest contributor to whatever success I have achieved in my life.

The other half of the credit of my success goes to my better half, our children and all other family members. My family – my wife Nandini, our son, Manas Tanksale, and daughter, Manjiri Tanksale – Jakhadi, has been extremely supportive of my efforts and has often sacrificed their own comforts – changing schools, homes and cities, content to living within the means I provided them and never demanding more - to adjust to my career transitions.

I am always thankful to my Mentors, bosses, colleagues and peers in the banking industry who have supported and enriched my learnings.

Once again I thank Mr V Leeladhar, Mr MV Nair and Mr K R Kamath for their consistent mentoring and the blessings through the Foreword they wrote for this book.

Above all this book would not have been written without the constant support and motivation of my dear friend Mandar Mhatre, Chief Revenue Officer, Formidium Corp. It was his suggestion, coupled with the initial efforts of my friend, Dr Svetlana Tatuskar, Director, Kohinoor Business School, that first started off this book and then the ongoing help and efforts of my friend and author Janhavi Samant, Senior Group

Head, Adfactors PR, and A K Roy Choudhary, Retd GM Punjab National Bank, that have led to the completion of this book.

Svetlana and I spent months discussing my career journey making a whole lot of notes. Janhavi took this effort forward by referring to these notes, collating the info and interactions and helped me put a structure – with chapters and taglines – to all this effort. I sincerely appreciate Svetlana and Janhavi's contribution and Mandar's encouragement to not give up on this project.

I thank all my prospective readers in advance. I would urge you to make the best use of my shared experience.

God Bless You.

Foreword

The Indian Banking industry, during the last 5 decades, has made long decisive strides, towards improving Customer Service, strengthening the financial position of the banks and introducing new financial products with adequate Risks Management Systems. Some of these steps are briefly covered below:

1. All bank branches, 50 years back were full of voluminous ledgers, stacked on the counters. Sometimes even the bank staff sitting behind the counters, giving services to the customer, were hidden and only their voices used to be heard by the customer. Every work including the calculation of interest used to be done manually using calculators. Even in larger branches, balancing of the books everyday, after the business hours, which was also done manually, and the entire staff would necessarily wait for the books to be tallied for the day.

2. As more and more people started using bank services, the bank management started feeling the need for computerisation, but there were many hurdles. The unions of the bank staff were strongly objecting to computerisation as they felt the computers, in due course, will replace the bank staff and reduce their members. Finally in late 1980s, after protracted negotiations, with the concurrence of the unions, some of the bank started installing huge computers with many of the processing parts of the machines deactivated as insisted by the unions. However it was only the beginning. Now with the core banking system in every bank, the customer service has improved everywhere and there is computerisation of virtually every activity. The major tiresome work of balancing of books has

become a by-product of the computer installed, coming out at the close of the business hours.

3. The Narsimham Committee recommendation were game changers of the Indian banking industry. As India liberalised its economy in 1991, it was felt that Banks are not performing efficiently. During economic crisis, it was recognised that banks have crucial role to play in the economy. The then Finance Minister Dr. Manmohan Singh set up a nine-member committee under the chairmanship of Mr. M Narsimham, the 13th Governor of Reserve Bank of India in 1991. A second committee known as Narsimham Committee – II was set up as follow up committee in 1998. The major recommendations made by the two committees became the strong foundations of the Indian Banking Industry. The Committee I suggested reduction of the very high Statutory Liquidity Ratio (SLR), suggested minimum Capital Adequacy Ratio, deregulation of interest rates, full disclosures of bank accounts and proper classification of assets. The Committee II covered reforms in the role of RBI, Government ownership of the banks, timelines for reduction of NPAs of the bank to 3% by 2002 and further increasing of Capital Adequacy Ratio. The banking regulator RBI pursued the implementation of these critical recommendations which led to the improvement of financial strength of each Banks very passionately.

4. Another initiative which has paid rich dividends is the strengthening and digitalisation of Indian payment and settlement system. I had the privilege of being in RBI where a decision to this effect was taken. We went about drafting a bill covering the payment and settlement and getting it approved by the Parliament. We formed a separate department in RBI to comprehensively handle the provisions or the Act. State-of-the-art data centres were set up in 3 centres, though Real Time Gross Settlement (RTGS) had just started, but only 2000 daily transactions were routed through by 3 banks (2 from private sector and 1 from a foreign bank). The setting

up of Unified Payments Interface (UPI) with its usage, safety and security with features like instant transfer of funds 24/7 started the advent of digital payment system in India. The RBI has been able to improve the global footprints of UPI and Rupay, to many countries. The payment and settlement system of the country is today considered to be one of the best in the world.

All these achievements were mainly due to the work of staff and officers of banks in thousands of bank branches located all over the country. The core teams set up at the Central office/ Regional offices of the banks fully supported the efforts of the staff and officers working in the branches. The technology companies in India supported the banks with robust hardware and software systems. Wherever, any investments in computerisation was to be decided, the first question before the Management was whether their staff/ officers would be able to use these machines and give better service to the Customers. Over the years the bank management saw that their staff/ officers are capable of handling the latest generation of computers.

I came across Mr. Mohan Tanksale, the author of this book in the year 2000 when I joined Union Bank of India as its Chairman and Managing Director.

Mohan, at that time, was a middle management officer working in one of the branches in Mumbai. A born leader, very passionate in his work, always customer centric, and he was always trying to achieve the targets given by his superiors. In addition, he was a God-fearing and highly religious person.

He started working closely with me and achieved promotions whenever there was a process where he was eligible for promotion. Thus, a young boy who had joined Central Bank of India as clerk to supplement the income of his family rose to become the Chairman and Managing Director of the Central Bank of India.

This book very vividly, in lucid English language explains the Indian Banking in the last 5 decades. I am sure young bankers and the students of the colleges/ institutions awaiting to become bankers will find the book very useful.

I wish Mohan and his book all the very best.

Vittaldas Leeladhar
Former Dy. Governor,
Reserve Bank of India.

Foreword

Much is known and being talked about the rapid strides made by Banks in India since their Nationalisation in 1969 till date and the different phases Banks went through during this period like mass banking, priority sector lending, steering economic liberalisation in the post-reform era, adopting prudential banking norms, computerisation and digitization, universal banking and going international. Unarguably such great achievements could be made possible due to the untiring and zealous efforts of a band of people in the Banks who were dedicated to the task given and who helmed the transformation initiatives at different points in time. Mr Mohan Tanksale can be easily counted among those *change agents* who contributed to the growth of the banks they were working for.

This trait of Mr Tanksale drew my attention within a few days of my taking over as CMD of Union Bank of India in April 2006. Mr Tanksale had just been promoted as General Manager of the Bank and was posted as the Field General Manager of the biggest Zone of the Bank in terms of size and business volume Mumbai. That was the time when Public Sector Banks in general and Union Bank in particular faced the dilemma of re-inventing themselves and re-strategizing to stay ahead of the competition and offer differentiated products and services and banking solutions. When I proposed to set in motion an ambitious transformation process for the bank named Project Nav Nirman, he was amongst the few in the top management team who took to the idea with great enthusiasm and played a pivotal role in the various initiatives like Core Banking solutions, centralization of Back Office Operations, third party products, Transaction Banking, forging strategic alliances, new brand identity, HR initiatives etc., to drive the transformation process. The result of these efforts are there for all to see – Union Bank, which was 11th among 14 banks nationalised, is counted among the top 5 Public Sector Banks in the country today.

Banking being essentially a service enterprise dealing in money, it is a bane of PSBs that decision makers / performers many times attract the attention of the central investigating agencies for wrong reasons and would have to face prolonged investigation / enquiry processes sapping the morale of the person concerned with cascading effects on those who work in his /her team. In such situations a true leader would not lose his poise and composure but would continue to work with undiminished enthusiasm towards the cause of the Bank and motivate his colleagues. This trait, I found in Mr. Tanksale when he found himself in such an unpleasant situation during my time. That he came out of the situation unscathed is a different story, but the amount of mental agony he experienced during the time could be imagined. But he did not allow that to have an impact on his enthusiastic spirit for the mission he was embarking upon.

What is amazing about Mr. Tanksale is that even after his retirement from active service he keeps himself relevant in the industry through his constant endeavour of re-skilling and re-learning and involving himself in all the new and emerging developments in the Banking and Technology. Thus, he is able to mentor and guide the young crop of bankers and entrepreneurs / startup ventures in the fintech world. An insatiable urge to learn new skills is one of the traits which I always admire in him.

I am happy that he chose to compile his rich banking expriences of over four decades in the form of a book aptly titled as " *Banking Beyond Borders*." In the book, he has vividly recollected the systematic changes commencing from the Branch expansion under Lead Bank Scheme in the '70s till the on-going digital revolution in all of which he has played crucial roles in the three banks he worked in and continues to play as board member/consultant /mentor to the companies and fintech start-ups. What is noteworthy about his work is that throughout, he has adopted a conversational style with lucid writing in simple English to reach a larger reader segment. Students of banking and finance as well as the aspiring business leaders can gain useful insights from the book that can help shape their careers. A book that deserves to be in the libraries of every Management School, College and University.

I wish his venture all success and wish him the best.

M V Nair
Former CMD,
Union Bank of India.

Foreword

People born in Independent India had the fortune of being witness to the transformation of the country in all facets of life. Banking is not an exception to this. It transformed from Ledgers, Cheques, Tokens to Paperless, Online and Offsite Banking. From the role of "collecting deposits for the purpose of lending" to a "financial supermarket" has been a great journey. It is worth documenting, lest it is forgotten.

I am happy that Mohan Tanksale, a hard core public sector banker has made a sincere attempt to capture this illustrious journey in the form of this book "Banking Beyond Borders."

The book is a testimony to the fact that "you dream, you believe, you act and you achieve."

Starting as a clerk and reaching to head a large Public Sector Bank and thereafter steering the industry body, Indian Banks' Association, as Chief Executive is almost half a century journey in banking.

In this book, Tanksale has not only captured his journey but also the transformation of the Banking Industry from Class banking to Mass banking during the period. It also covers the way Technology changed the industry and helped to reach out to the people who were kept out of the privilege of having a Bank account. It also captures the journey of the customer from a Branch Customer to a Bank Customer. The book serves as a reference guide on the development of banking in India over the last five decades.

Being a meticulous record keeper of events, Tanksale has captured the progress of Indian Banking while narrating his own career progression.

As a totally positive person, he has brought out how to look at challenges and convert them into opportunities. Banking is all about touching the lives of the people and making difference to their lives. An accomplished banker will always have scores of people remembering how he was instrumental in changing their lives – be it customers or staff.

A "Never say Die" person, Tanksale has narrated how to build units to Institutions and how the Team responds if you empower them and give them the freedom to operate while owning up their failures as a true leader. In academic parlance, Banking is always referred to as Banking Law and Practice. It means that consistently followed Practice attains the position of Law. Tanksale, as a practicing banker, has tried to collate his experiences and presented it through this book for the benefit of larger audience.

I am sure that the Book makes an interesting reading not only to the Bankers but also to people who pursue their career in other fields. No book can provide a solution to all the problems of the readers. But it can create confidence in the readers to handle any situation they encounter. I am sure that Banking Beyond Borders is one such book.

While I compliment Tanksale for bringing out this book, I wish all the readers a Happy Reading.

K R Kamath
Former CMD,
Punjab National Bank.

Preface

Starting a new account

Business and life are like a bank account – you can't take out more than you put in.
- Author and publisher William Feather

It is perhaps this need that has prompted me to put together this book. I entered the banking industry as a 19-and half-year old intern in Central Bank of India in 1973 and ended up building my life, purpose and spiritual calling around the hub of this vibrant industry. As a banker whose career over four decades spanned from clerical work in Central Bank Of India to the Chairmanship of Central Bank of India and further heading the Indian Banks' Association as Chief Executive, I have been both a witness and contributor to the staggering growth of the banking industry and the central role it has played in the economic growth of India as an economic superpower.

When I started my internship in banking as a youth, it was with the intention of supporting my father with his financial goals. On the very first day as a clerk in Central Bank of India, I was extremely excited with the opportunity I was provided. A simple job like that, paying Rs 400 per month, could ease the financial challenges my parents were facing and could subsidise my own further education. I started with this enthusiasm and excitement to excel at this job right from the beginning.

Through so many decades, the banking industry has been viewed as an easy, stable, safe and preferred employer for the Indian middle-class. At the time I joined, there were no computers, no core banking; we had to work with huge ledgers, sit for hours balancing books on monthly and quarterly closing working days. And we had to rely on our memory and manual calculations to get all the work right. In those days, youngsters who were academically competent and good with their mathematical skills were encouraged to pursue banking as a career. A comfortable working environment, fixed predictable work hours, steady income with eligibility for quick home and personal loans, promotions at regular intervals, banking meant a safe, comfortable urban life for a youth like me, who was expected to support my family financially as soon as I graduated.

Well, as you shall see, safe, comfortable and predictable would be the last adjectives I would use to describe my career.

Little did I know that my career arc would take me through some very exciting and historic developments in the industry that would allow me to contribute fruitfully to the India story that we now see. Some of these opportunities were handed to me by virtue of the times I lived in. Computerisation, liberalisation and privatisation were a boon to the Indian economy and opened the world up for the country. But there were many opportunities also which I grabbed with both hands. Being proactive in adapting to change, being on the lookout for the right opportunities, taking advantage of every single opportunity to learn, honing my networking skills, making the right career moves at the right time, choosing the long, rough but exciting path over the safe and smooth road have all ensured that my journey over the last five decades has always been most exciting.

It is these experiences that I would like to share with young banking professionals as learnings from a successful and spiritually fulfilling innings in this industry. This is how I prefer to give back to the career that has given me so much.

In hindsight, it is easier to gloss over failures and glamourise successful decisions. However that is not the aim of this project.

As a consultant to various finance start-up initiatives and a member of various Boards and Committees, I am privy to working closely with many youngsters in today's times. It is wonderful to observe the perspective of my young colleagues, who have grown up with such quick access to computers, technology and search engines. They have a unique approach to their careers and their own lives rather than the trial and error methods that my generation applied to their lives.

Millenials today live and experience their lives fully and more fulfillingly than my generation ever did. The intense VUCA (Volatility, Uncertainty, Complexity and Ambiguity) nature of the world of banking and finance also renders much of my academic knowledge quite redundant. But even as India, with its demographic and geographic diversity, adapts to cutting edge, digital technology, with such speed, it still remains firmly old-world and conventional in its heart.

Some of my grassroots wisdom and old school reflections may help you with a robust understanding of what banking means to our economy and the role it has played in the progress of our country. And therefore, I urge my young readers to read the life lessons that I share not as a sermon or a lecture series, but rather as a sharing of meaningful experiences that may guide you in your banking career in the future.

Chapter 1

The Very First Deposit

So let me begin at the beginning.

I was academically a strong student. I scored 80% in 11th. I had chosen Science and would usually score well in Maths. I could have got into engineering very easily. But the financial situation at home was not very conducive to me studying engineering. My father was on the verge of retirement and I was expected to support him in his domestic responsibilities. So I enrolled for B.Sc in Physics, Chemistry and Maths. This was between 1969 to 1972. In 1972, I graduated with Third position in Bhopal University with a National Scholarship. As luck would have it, I got admission for post graduate course in applied chemistry at Maulana Azad College of Technology, Bhopal. We were only five students and we had wonderful mentoring from professors. I had been working on my English writing skills since I had studied in Hindi medium school. On the side, I had also enrolled for Russian studies. It was a two year diploma and I excelled very well.

At the time, it was a very common thing for graduates to appear for banking exams. The banking industry was nationalised in 1969. The 70s were a time of rapid growth. I followed suit with many of my middle-class friends to appear for banking exams for clerical positions. At the time, there were many opportunities to grow from clerical to managerial positions in banking through internal tests and exams. I got an appointment letter in January 1973, to work as a clerk in Central Bank of India.

My father and my teachers were totally disappointed with a bright student like me taking up a clerical job. Their aspiration was that I should appear for competitive exams like those for probationary officers or the civil services. But I was somehow quite convinced with the step I was taking. I didn't look at the position as that of a lowly clerk. I felt that there was an inner calling that this stint would unlock a very big opportunity for me. I was convinced that, despite the position, I would somehow make this work. This instinct has served me in good stead over the years.

I moved out of the college, much to the consternation of my professors and elders, and started as a clerk with the Central Bank Of India.

My initial responsibility was very simple. Since I was a science student, I was given the job of compiling statistical information. In those days, there was no technology or tools available to bankers. There was only a calculator. I was good at calculations and my job was to work with the statistics department. I approached my assignment with a lot of enthusiasm. I was extremely happy that the salary the job offered me helped me support my family and my siblings' education.

I had an elder brother who had started work in the Insurance sector where the income wasn't certain. I learnt as much as I could on the job. But I was very much aware that this was not my destination. This was only a point on a much longer and exciting journey. And although I wasn't clear what my dreams and aspirations were at that particular point of time, I was clear that this job would lead to bigger achievements later in my career.

So I was preparing for the exam for probationary officers for State Bank Of India while I worked. There were two reasons for this: The first, of course, was our family's financial constraints. Secondly, it was the advice given by my father's friend Mr M B Deshmukh, who was with SBI at the time and who retired as Managing Director. He was in-charge of Bhopal local head office; my dad had consulted him about a career in banking for me before, I had joined Central Bank. Mr Deshmukh advised me to go ahead with the job but to appear for clerical/ probationary officer exams in SBI as well. At that time, SBI offered excellent opportunities for growth and promotions every 3–4 years.

I appeared for the exam and within 3–4 months I got appointed to State Bank of India as a clerk. However, given my experience and performance in the Russian Studies diploma, I was chosen to do a one-month teacher training course in Moscow. This was in 1973; I was only 20.

It was a wonderful opportunity where I got to meet teachers from across the world and interact with them. India had strong relations with the USSR. My institution was affiliated to the Indo-Soviet Cultural Association, India. The Vaidyas were the founders of Dr A V Baliga Institute of Russian Studies in Bhopal and also my mentors and teachers.

I was permitted by SBI to join them after concluding my training in Moscow. I returned from there to join as a clerk at State Bank of India in July 1973. SBI was a whole new world of learning. All said and done, the Central Bank was smaller as compared to the State Bank. SBI had a much wider scope; they also offered opportunities for bright students to write exams and get promotions as Trainee Officers. I could have waited to join as an officer, but I joined as a clerk. By this time, perhaps fuelled by confidence of being able to do the job and of doing the right thing by my family, I had a sort of certainty that I was on the right path in my career.

My father, who was himself a Superintendent in the Registrar office, Madhya Pradesh, had very high ambitions for me. He kept encouraging me to pursue my studies. My schooling was in Hindi language. Because of this, my spoken and written English was not very good. He therefore pushed me to pursue an MA in English Literature so as to perfect my English skills and appear for IAS exams.

By the time I completed BSc, I won Rs 1000 as a scholarship. I used this money to buy a bike. In those days, my schedule as a student and a clerk in SBI was extremely hectic. I would leave the house at 6.30 a.m. to attend college upto 9.30 a.m., then rush to the office by 10.30 a.m.. In SBI, I was very well accepted as a team member; my superiors found me efficient, committed and sincere. Over the months I worked there, my superiors also encouraged me to take the Certified Associate of Institute of Indian Banking (CAIIB) exams in banking..

Book-keeping, Accounting and Economics were subjects that were completely foreign to me. I didn't know anything about these subjects. But the way SBI incentivised this was that every completed module of the CAIIB exam came with an increment. And so I persevered and worked hard and was able to complete CAIIB Part 1 at one go and enjoy the financial benefits that came with it. I was also giving Probationary Officer exams of other banks on the side.

I cleared that exam in Jan 1974 for Union Bank of India. That had its own set of processes for hiring and soon I was appointed as Probationary Officer in Union Bank in August 1974. So I resigned from SBI and joined Union Bank.

But that one year at SBI gave me a lot of learning. Especially MIS, deposits, assets, advances, general ledger accounts etc; we did all that work manually. Computerisation was introduced in banking only after 1988.

This clerical work was very focused and extremely detail-oriented. We had to sit and total 20–30 items at a time. My math skills were good and I was one of the preferred valued clerks to the officers in my office. I was never treated or considered as a clerk and my work was very well recognised and appreciated. In fact, the officers who worked with me throughout the early phase of my career only encouraged me to prepare for exams and study further.

All in all, I spent a lot of time in early couple of years assimilating and absorbing my initial learnings and preparing myself with banking exams and promotions that brought me to Union Bank of India, Gwalior as an officer in 1974.

Today, when I pause to think about it, I realise that there were many reasons that I was able to build so much equity with my managers in such little time. Let me outline them:

Don't wait for opportunity to knock; keep the door open so you can respond immediately. To the reader, my swift job changes in the early years of my career may seem disconcerting. I would say that these job shifts had a lot to do with spotting the best learning opportunities, whether academic or professional, and broadening my world view. For instance, participating in a month-long teachers training programme in Moscow or continuing with an MA in English Literature or attempting the Probationary Officers' exams or the CAIIB exam while I was doing a full-time job. Because I studied on the side, I was constantly able to look at available opportunities. This enabled me to become one of the youngest Branch Managers at the age of 23 in Union Bank of India.

Approach all work with an open mind. I was an academically bright student. I passed all my tests with flying colours. Even when I was a clerk, I approached all assignments diligently and with an open mind. When I started on my first job as an officer, I learnt banking from Mr Pandey, a daftari at our Union Bank branch. A daftari is the head peon of the branch, who maintains all records. What are these vouchers; why are they colour coded; how do you file the paperwork; all these things I learnt from Pandeyji. There have been times after I became a Branch Manager, while setting up a new branch in a small town, that I have had to do even the peon and cleaner's job! However small the job, I always learnt to deliver it in the best way possible.

Maximise your learning. It is important to put your intelligence in the mix and see the magic happen. I have seen too many of my peers and even young bankers get bogged down by the process and rut in their day-to-day work without trying to add value and intelligence to what they deliver. Then there were the trainings that the bank sent me to regularly that also proved to be very helpful in learning the ropes. In that induction training as Probationary Officers, we not only learnt how to do the job but also how to network and establish professional relationships.

Develop a rational, analytical approach to your work. I have seen too many youngsters take their work and even mistakes too personally. This includes reactions to what their boss says or does. One should always develop the skill to evaluate a situation or feedback or issue in an independent manner. If a boss says something, do not react immediately and emotionally. Take the time to study the situation and then respond in an objective manner. Consider if a different solution may work and then discuss it with the boss in a calm and rational manner. Being a yes-man won't help. You need to have the courage to disagree rationally as well.

Develop a multi-faceted personality. While it is important that we learn how to 'do' the job efficiently; we must also learn to polish other aspects of our personality. I played badminton. I was part of the Peace Corps where I learnt English speaking because of a good British teacher. I used to be an NCC cadet; I served as Cadet Captain. This can do wonderful things for our professional confidence as it also builds an independent network of social contacts which has paid rich dividends to me over the decades. I was involved in dramatics as well. I remember that we had once performed a play on stage in my school in which my job was to bring a live donkey on to the stage! Imagine that!

The above learnings helped me navigate my way as a newly minted officer at Union Bank in Gwalior and eventually led me to be appointed as a Branch Manager in just two years. This road was not smooth.

As a newly minted officer, my role underwent a tremendous shift in terms of the deliverables expected of me and went on to teach me some important lessons in banking.

Chapter 2

The Officer Life

As stated earlier, I joined the Gwalior branch of Union Bank of India as an officer in August 1974. This stint in Gwalior proved to be a major turning point in my life, not just professionally but also personally. There were a few reasons for this. Let me expand on them.

Having come from clerical and number-crunching experience from two banks, I was quick to catch on in this new position. At the time, my branch manager and boss was late Mr A.B. Gujarati. He placed his faith in me and gave me responsibilities early on. In fact within just three to four weeks, he decided to appoint me as a Relationship Manager for all the prime accounts of the branch.

Prime accounts for the branch meant accounts of important people, handling important decisions relating to finance. I began with one Mr D P Mandelia, who was a Financial Advisor to none other than industrialist Mr G D Birla. The Birlas had a huge set-up with Gwalior Rayon Industries and J C Mills in the city and carried lot of clout. Mr Mandelia had overdraft limit against shares in our branch jointly with his wife Indumati Mandelia. The other big account was the Gupta family account; it was a family of advocates, one of who retired as a High Court judge from Madhya Pradesh eventually.

Managing these key accounts would mean ensuring that their banking needs were met; to ensure that they received their interest certificates on time, that their term deposits were renewed and whatever facilities they required were promptly delivered. Soon after this, Mr Gujarati put me in charge of industrial advances as well.

After a short while, our Branch Accountant was promoted and transferred out and there was no replacement of the Accountant. So, in my probationary period itself, I got the chance to be an Accountant for my branch. Now the Accountant of a branch is the second in command, right after the Branch Manager. These were some big opportunities for a new probationary officer like me. In those days, we didn't have any computers to do the computing or the balance sheets or tallying. We had to do it all manually. So the half-yearly closing of accounts, which includes interest calculations, application, posting of entries, balancing of books, would be an exhausting, time-consuming process. We would have to stay in the office as late as 2 am to 3 am and return back early in the morning. In those days, clerks were paid overtime for these days on which they worked late.

The employees' union was quite active in demanding overtime. Now, in 1975, when the Emergency was imposed by Mrs Indira Gandhi, banks declared that payment for overtime would be stopped. Since clerks did not get overtime, they would push off home once their timings were done. Officers weren't paid any overtime so we had to sit back and finish whatever work needed to be done. In fact the officers of our branch did all the clerical work most efficiently. This didn't go well with the union leaders at all. One night at 2 am, I had finished my work and was about to go home. I came out of the branch to find that the tyres of my scooter had been punctured! I was in a fix. It was too late to get the tyres repaired or to catch a taxi or auto rickshaw home. This was probably done by one of the local union leaders out of vengeance to teach us a lesson. I quietly turned back into the office and spent the night there. In the morning, I woke up and bathed in the office itself and started working again.

In a way, this stint as an officer proved to be rich with learnings. Let me outline some of them:

Let your boss worry over your potential. You grab every opportunity he sends your way. It was an incredible opportunity for me. As is my nature, I didn't spend this time worrying over whether I was skilled enough to fulfill this responsibility. Clearly my boss saw some potential in me to give me this profile. So I trusted his instinct and faith in me. So I spent this time upskilling myself and learning everything related to relationship management and diplomacy and processes that my new position would require of me.

Banking is not lending so much as problem-solving. Bankers make the mistake of believing that they are lenders. But that is not true at all. People need to borrow money in order to solve their problems. A banker therefore needs to view every borrowing or investment transaction as a customer problem and find the most effective solution to that problem. The important thing is therefore to understand the need of the customer and their business really well. Clients need to think of you as a partner rather than a lender. Relationship management taught me to interact with the customer with humility and a problem-solving approach. This helped my clients to trust me and my advice. The real dividends came when they started referring me to their friends and family for banking business.

This stint also brought home to me a crucial piece of learning about banking. Credit monitoring is the most important aspect of banking. And it has taught me a big lesson. I was the banker for a manufacturing unit which was into the business of importing plastic waste and converting it into sheets and pipes, etc. Their paperwork was perfect and I had done my due diligence very thoroughly. However during the audits, we discovered some fraud in their pledge accounts. I was very surprised that a client who had such flawless operation in accounts and such a good reputation could have committed this. I was fortunate that this happened during my very initial years, because it proved to me the importance of credit monitoring.

Banking goes beyond paperwork. Lack of monitoring leads to frauds. And therefore monitoring borrowers and their businesses is most important. This monitoring has to go beyond paperwork. A banker has to step out and visit a client's business or place of work or shop and subtly verify whatever has been submitted in the paperwork. Check the accounts, the spending; understand the business and where the money is being used. Monitoring needs to be on the spot and not on paper.

Some of these lessons are the reason I got promoted to Branch Manager within just two years. But some of these lessons were not just professional in nature. On a personal front, my family too played a huge role in my growth and perspective towards my career.

I have already shared that I was taking on some of my family responsibilities of my father. By the time I was appointed as probationary officer in Gwalior, my father had already retired. At the time, the entire family (my mother, father and two brothers) all decided to shift from Bhopal to Gwalior with me. When I think of it now, it can't have been easy to have shifted lock, stock and barrel, change schools and colleges for my siblings and so on just for a job posting. But my family has always been totally encouraging and supportive towards my dreams in every way possible.

Actually my parents were very simple people. My father was a superintendent in the Government Registrar's office and my mother was a homemaker. But both of them worked very hard to support and help not only their own children but even their relatives, friends, neighbours as well. As far as I can remember, there would be always be a job-seeking or student cousin, uncle or aunt or two living in our house. My dad has helped with the marriages of many of my cousins.

I have seen my father interact with the IAS officers and other bureaucrats around him. He was very well-respected by his superiors; they valued his opinions and experiences. He also started his career as a clerk but then he completed his degree as a doctor of Homeopathy. He took great pride in calling himself Dr V V Tanksale. My mother was also an extremely respected woman. She must have barely studied till 4th or 5th standard. But she would recite Das Bodh, a spiritual treatise by renowned saint Shri Ramdas Swamy like an expert. For nine days of the Das Navami, she would narrate the story of Samarth Ram Das in sermons for the entire community. She was also very active in the Mahila mandal and the Ganesh mandal in our neighbourhood. They both are no more, but I realise that it is my upbringing and conditioning that have formed the core of my values as a professional.

Believe in your dreams. One belief they had was to always believe in dreams. They both grew up in a lower income household, but they were always committed to the betterment, growth and education of everyone around them. When I got the chance to go to Moscow for the teacher training, I was told that I would have to bear the cost of the one-way airfare on my own. I was worried; in those days the ticket cost Rs 3000–4000 and I wasn't sure where we would get the money from. But my father was adamant that I should go and he borrowed money against his provident fund so I would be able to go abroad. It was the same when they all shifted so readily from Bhopal to come set up with me in Gwalior. Within two years, I was promoted to Branch Manager to set up a new branch in Sidhi district of Madhya Pradesh. Although, it would again require them to shift, my family was extremely supportive of my dreams. After my marriage in 1980, my wife also continued to be invested in my growth. In the times before computerisation, she also sat with me and helped me with the Branch Balance Sheets and Ledgers when the need arose.

Practise humility. Another of their values was humility. Whatever the status and background of the person they spoke to, they would always be respectful. That is how my father built such a supportive network of relationships through his career. This helped me tremendously when I took up relationship management and also when I became manager and started dealing with my own team.

Always be helpful. Helpfulness was another trait they both shared. My father has financially contributed to the education and marriages of several of his own brothers and sisters and nephews and nieces. As a homeopathy practitioner, he was always happy to be dispensing free medicines to those needy around them. Both of them were extremely active in fundraising and organising the construction of the Datt Mandir temple, which has now become such a large charitable entity in Bhopal.

To be honest, I would not have been able to take the huge strides I did in my career if it were not for the support of all my family. This quality of caring for the community, giving back to it in whatever way possible, was inherent in my parents. And it was programmed into me right from my childhood. When I now think about it, this quality is what fostered the spirit of customer-centricity as a core value inside me. This is what my transfer as Branch Manager to a small district like Sidhi and navigating its community and banking issues taught me about this concept.

Chapter 3

Sidhi Baat

Experts may have written several books on understanding and enhancing customer satisfaction but at its core, customer-centricity in banking is all about being committed to solving problems and enabling the growth of the customer.

Sidhi was a long way away from my home in Bhopal. Sidhi is a small district, almost 800 kms from Gwalior, 600 kms from Bhopal and it is adjoining the Mirazapur district of Uttar Pradesh.

I was relatively young and I came to Sidhi in the September of 1976 determined to be the best branch manager ever. The branch managership was for a new branch to be set up in a place called Morva, which is in Sidhi. This area was located in the Central Coalfields Limited project area of Singrauli. This was also the first Regional Headquarters for Coal India Ltd.

Since my initial banking experience was limited to Bhopal and Gwalior, the Morva experience was quite an eye-opener for me. As the first branch manager, I had to start from ground zero.

When I say ground zero, I mean it literally. I had nothing apart from the licence to open the branch in that area. At the time, Rewa was the district from where the Development Manager, who controlled those districts, would operate from. So I first reported to my Development Manager there. It was late Dr J Mishra; he was a professor at Orissa

University for agriculture. He had joined the bank as a senior officer and he turned out to be a wonderful mentor to me. He was extremely enthused about this opportunity for me. I remember him taking me around 200 kms to Morva in his jeep and showing me around the place. He took me around to check out possible office premises. Eventually, we found a 200-odd sq ft area.

He advised me to put in 2–3 proposals and negotiate for a good rate too.

On the day of the opening, we did not even have a peon! I had hired a temporary person for rudimentary cleaning, and I did the rest of the clearing up of the premises myself. At the time, I was living in a God-forsaken lodge too.

It was a very challenging time for me. I was not only new to the area but also completely lacked the know-how of how small towns operated. I had only worked as an officer till then. I had been only responsible for my performance so far. Now I had to bear the responsibility for my entire team. Besides, everything from new business development, relationship management, meeting deadlines and so on had to be juggled together. My work so far has been task-oriented and very specific. It seemed like a very tough challenge at the time. This was not something I could have learnt in college or in a class. This was practical managerial know-how of which I had no experience till then.

Thankfully, my academic nature came to my rescue. Morva was where the Central Coalfields Ltd (CCL) had their regional headquarters. There were around 4–5 projects in that area and the whole ecosystem of Morva was built around these projects. This was unlike other cities which developed organically. I took some time to understand my audience and what their banking needs might be.

Let me enumerate some of the lessons I learnt while doing business development and marketing of my new branch in Morva.

Understanding the social fabric of the area. There were a lot of educated people who were employed by the Coalfield projects and the Central school was at the centre of the social network. Early on I realised that blending into that social fabric would help me make an impression. My refined approach, English speaking and relationship management skills helped. Bankers are always wondering about how to raise the retail deposits in a branch. Well, I decided to begin by targeting the school first. I canvassed the salary accounts of all the teachers at the Central school. Every month, salaries would be disbursed from my bank. The amount may not have been much, but I knew that the school was very influential in the social system there.

Start them young. In small towns, it is the youth that are more receptive to change in social behaviour. That year, Union Bank had introduced the School Bank Scheme. Children above 10 were allowed to open a minor account. They were gifted a red cash box with keys at the time of account opening. They had to take home this cash box and save whatever cash and coins they got and then take the money in the box once a month to deposit in their accounts. The keys to their cash box would be with me. I would open the cash box and deposit whatever cash there was in it. You won't believe the response we got for this scheme. But the wonder of this idea was: the red cash box at home would be seen by the parents every day. Besides, every time a child comes to the bank, the parents would also come. This made a tremendous impact on the number of accounts opened. I remember canvassing for these accounts home to home.

Some work and some play. I didn't do it with much awareness at that time. But playing badminton helped me develop a lot of business. The Central Coalfields had a sports club where I went to play badminton. I was quite a good player and became very popular there. Many engineers came to play at the club too. And my popularity helped me market the bank to them. They opened their personal accounts at our branch.

Understand your customer. When I had spent a little time observing the social dynamics in Morva, I realised that, outside the projects, I had two kinds of customers. One was a group of contractors; it was a group of approved vendors. They had financial papers on the basis of which they could access loans and credit. But the other was a group of retailers; the kirana shops, garment shops, hardware shops. They all deserved credit but they had no papers to show. It was a big problem. They needed another solution. You will not believe what I did. Since I knew the basics of accounting and was used to working with balance sheets, I decided to help them prepare their documentation. Most of these shopkeepers only kept sales records. I asked them to add up all the sales records and purchase records every month. Then I would do an assessment of their stock and look at their expenses and earnings. I would prepare a sort of rough balance sheet. I would interview and record receivables and payables and created their balance sheets myself. Based on this, the bank could offer them a credit line. I replicated the same for the contractors. Of course, these lendings would only be in thousands but it helped a lot of people.

My branch management experience in Morva actually taught me that banking has a much larger role to play in our society than just saving, borrowing and lending. For instance, I could do something for small business owners and traders. But what could be done for farmers? And what would banking in an agricultural country like India be without agricultural finance?

In India there were some very important programmes which were driven by government under nationalisation. These were the Integrated Rural Development Programme and the Lead Bank Scheme. In the Lead Bank Scheme, every nationalised bank is given the responsibility of some districts in the country. We, at the Union Bank, were the Lead Bank for Sidhi district. In those days, we had to create a District Credit Plan to explain to our bosses what our plans were for developing banking in that district. Under the aegis of the Sarvangin Gram Vikas

Yojana, we had to adopt villages to enable their overall development. For this work, I visited many villages and met farmers. Till then, I had no idea what an Indian village was or how they operated.

I had to begin right from the beginning; Kharif and Rabi crops, irrigation, harvesting, seeds, pumps, farming implements etc. After talking to them, I realised that individual land sizes are very small and therefore commercially non-viable. The cost of a diesel pump is high, so it cannot be bought by a single small farmer. I would then recommend 3–4 nearby farmers to borrow together to buy a diesel pump.

It was in 1977 itself that I started reading up on collective farming. And it is a subject that I find fascinating even now. Collective farming has not really picked up in India but I believe it is the solution to agricultural finance. I will speak more about this subject later.

As I got the lay of the land and started setting up a base in Morva, one of the most influential contacts I made in Sidhi was one, Mr PK Bhattacharya, who was introduced to me by my boss. Mr Bhattacharya was in charge of the Renu Sagar Power Company Ropeways, which was transporting coal from the coal mines at Singrauli to Renu Sagar where the thermal power plant was located. He was an Engineer from Dhaka University. He was truly like an elder brother; his wife still calls me *'Bhaiyya.'*

He offered me a small place to live in and supported me in every way possible. When he saw that I was focusing on business development, he introduced me to all of his contacts at the Renu Sagar Power Co as well as Hindalco in Mirzapur district. This is how I began working with Hindalco; can you imagine a rank manager like me extending Rs 5 crore line of credit to Hindalco for bill discounting in 1977!

My contact, Mr RA Agarwal, was in charge of Hindalco. Signing up these accounts was a real turning point for me in my career. These helped me garner further support from the ecosystem in Sidhi. It helped me a big way in getting business from contractors from Ranchi, Allahabad and Railways to whom I issued bank guarantees. These were opportunities waiting to be picked up. I just developed the necessary networking skills to take charge and deliver these jobs.

Those were exciting days. Although the most fortuitous part happened in 1978–1979. That year, the Government of India decided to set up a Thermal Power Plant in Singrauli because of the coalfields in the area. They made a huge land acquisition in that area and in that process asked Union Bank to open a branch there. This branch was a landmark one; Shakti Nagar is one of the most important power generation hubs in India. We call it the Shakti Nagar branch.

The most important part of this stint was that it had me exercising my creativity for unique marketing ideas to win more accounts. My target was to be the dominant banker in the area. We already had Allahabad Bank, as the previous lead bank, and the State Bank Of India there, so there was serious competition.

Become more visible. I realised visibility was important when my solo branch was competing with big banks with an extensive reach. My social networking at the CCL Club helped me be more visible in the customer base of officers and engineers. Then I went further, got the lay of the land and talked to people as a representative of the bank. I realised one way to connect with people was to sponsor cultural events in the area. Over time, I observed that there were 4 coal fields around Singrauli. I saw that there could be a huge opportunity in this area and requested my bosses to open 4–5 more branches there. This helped Union Bank become quite visible in the area. When a bank branch is visible in many places, it automatically serves as a reminder to prospective clients about its availability.

Live your company ethos. I tried one simple experiment. Union Bank of India had a rising sun as its logo and called itself 'Good people to bank with' as a tagline. I decided to live that tagline. I started visiting people door to door like a salesman and opened zero-balance accounts for them. Zero balance accounts was not such a popular funda back then. I even went to the houses on the outskirts of the town and villages. I showed people publicity videos and networked a lot in those circles. We probably mobilised the highest deposits in those couple of years.

Connect with people at their level. If it was a shopkeeper, I would sit in his shop and talk about whatever was important to him. If it was a contractor, I would sit across a bike and visit his project site and have tea together. If it was a senior executive from Renu Sagar or Hindalco, I would sit across a table and chat with him too. Perhaps it was my easygoing nature, approach or it was my knowledge, but I could connect very quickly with people. This helped me understand their lives and their business problems better. One must think about how to add value to the business of the customer. Unless you have a win-win proposition, you don't have a business transaction. This helped me network too. As branch manager, I got the opportunity to interact with the Collector of Sidhi, Mr Ajit Jogi IAS and later Mr Bose IAS. Because of my engagement at the district level consultative committee, I developed a very congenial relationship till Mr Jogi joined politics and then he was elected Chief Minister of Chhatisgarh and Mr Bose, who retired as Revenue Secretary of Government of India. Mr Parshuram, who retired as Chief Secretary of Madhya Pradesh, was actually my counterpart initially in Rewa district in 1979 and later at the State level Banker's Committee Madhya Pradesh from 2011 to 2013 in my capacity as Chairman of Central Bank. It is important to blend into the cultural and network ecosystem of your branch.

Focus on finding solutions to your customer's issues. My most common observation is that bankers rigidly hold on to the procedure and formalities rather than solving the customer's problem. Very often, bankers do not mind letting go of a relationship rather than adjusting their own paperwork needs. A lot of bankers are scared to go that extra mile for a client for fear that their paperwork will increase. I believe that paperwork exists for the customer; it can't exist at the cost of the customer. Therefore, bankers have to keep an open solution-oriented mind. You should be interested in finding out more. So, whether it was helping my customers prepare their documentation or even balance sheets or canvassing for teachers and zero-balance accounts, wanting to solve clients' problems did work for me.

When I eventually became Chairman of Central Bank in 2011, I made it a point to visit the branch and town that gave a solid foundation to my career. I visited the Morva and Shakti Nagar branch, which is now in a big building, and did a few customer meetings too. I also visited Hindalco and the Renu Sagar Power Co. It was a wonderful experience; I had visited this area after 40 years and helped me see my past efforts come to fruition. It was like I had come a full circle!

It was only three years, but almost a lifetime of experience as a first-time Manager. When the bank recognised my performance and posted me at the district headquarters branch at Rewa, I was sorry to let go of all the connections I had made in Morva. My clients were most apprehensive if my successor would also be as helpful as me.

As in Morva, I did the complete survey of opportunities to grow our banking business at Rewa. I identified the top customers from each category of business and industry in the area and met with them to understand what their business needs were. Besides I also developed relationships with various institutions like the local municipal corporations, nearby schools and colleges, hospitals and developed the banking business. This effort was well-recognised by my superiors in 1982 and helped me for further elevation in the cadre by promoting me as General Manager of Rewa Sidhi Grameen Bank, a Regional Rural Bank sponsored by Union Bank of India

Another reason this stint at Rewa proved to be remarkable for me is because I also got married in 1980. I was pursuing part 2 of the CAIIB exams and MA English finals. I also wanted to become the most successful branch manager, so you can imagine my schedule. But my wife was such a huge support. She was extremely understanding of my work and educational commitments. Sometimes she would even lend a hand with my actual banking work. In those days, when we had to balance the books at the end of the month, we had to work on a ledger and the balance had to be called out on it and recorded. At times, I would bring it home and my wife would call up the numbers and I would note them down. I passed the CAIIB exams and won two increments for the same, which helped my financial position as well. I would say her contribution has been most invaluable during this momentous phase of my life.

Apart from her firm support, it was the blessings of all the local friends and connections I had made that held me in good stead in the next phase of my career, which was spurred on by computerisation and then by the great wave of liberalisation.

Chapter 4

Tech Start

Computerisation was introduced in Indian banking in 1988. The Dr Rangarajan committee was set up to implement this exercise in different banks. To some extent, some technological initiatives had already made an entry into banks in the back offices. But computerisation refers to mainly branch computerisation. At the time, MIS, compilation and aggregation of information was mainly done on computers. Although it started in 1988, it took Union Bank till 2007 to conclude core banking and for all branches to be computerised.

The initial couple of years the computerisation process was extremely slow and arduous. However it was actually the fortuitous three-pronged landmark event of Liberalisation, Privatisation and Globalisation that helped truly speed up the process of computerisation in banking.

Indian banking got its most important push through privatisation with the setting up of private banks. Now these banks, ICICI Bank and Axis Bank, erstwhile UTI Bank, were computerised on day one of their operations. Till the 90s, we were filling up passbooks, calculating interest by hand.

There was simply no comparison between the service of a computerised bank, where everything could be done at the click of a finger, and a bank where all operations were manual.

I believe computerisation needs to be viewed from a dual perspective. First, the technology tremendously helped the bank's operational efficiency. Secondly, it tangibly improved customer service. Till the 90s, we did book balancing, statement of accounts, physical balance sheets manually; it was all a lot of needless labour. But when computerisation happened, bankers saw huge benefits of serving customers more efficiently than ever before. Out there, the current account ledger was 1300 pages thick; it was one and half feet wide and two and a half feet long. Lifting that itself was a big exercise.

By doing away with a lot of unproductive labour and potential for manual error, computerisation brought about a sea change in the banking world. Yet, it took very long for bankers to see it for the boon it was.

Predominantly, it was the unions who feared that there would be tremendous job losses with the advent of computerisation. At the time, clerical staff were paid overtime for working extra hours; that added significantly to their incomes. Time-saving technology would have a huge impact on their earnings. So the first push-back came from the Unions. It is of course now historically proven that there were no job losses because of computerization. But at that time, no one believed this.

But they couldn't protest it too much either because our banks now had to compete with fully computerised technologically savvy private banks which offered core banking solutions right from the beginning. So it was a question of survival.

For instance, if a customer asked for a statement of accounts in the good old days, my clerk would have to write it by hand. They would take the debit summation and credit summation and then see whether the balance is correct. There would be mistakes, reiterations and so on.

In a private bank, the data is available at the click of a button and you got a statement for whatever period you want.

Hence, looking at the service of private banks, public sector banks were forced to adapt in order to survive. They had to adapt and learn new technology if they needed to retain their clients. Thus there was rapid adoption post 1994.

When Union bank started undergoing computerisation, they first started a separate department, the Computer Policy and Placement department (CPPD). We hired the relevant people from the open market and started implementing the project. Initially, it was just monitors given at the branch level, basis the importance and the volume of business, and branches were computerised individually. I was posted at the Arera Colony branch in Bhopal at the time this happened in 1990–1991.

Computerisation was to entirely change the way we conducted banking and it was natural for many bankers to feel apprehensive of those changes. Typically youngsters inducted into banking in the 70s and 80s were quite adaptive to the technological changes. The senior officers, the managers, who had joined banking pre-nationalisation, took a little more time to adjust.

However I chose to take these transformative technology in a positive manner. The ease of functioning was tremendous. As an officer who did not earn any overtime, I often found myself taking home work on weekends and holidays. Like I have mentioned, even my wife had to pitch in and help me.

At the time, our bank incentivised its officers to learn computers. I did a three-month diploma in computers which the bank paid for. It was a new way to approaching work that we had been doing for years.

I realised that during this kind of transformation, I must understand and learn so that I could guide and motivate my branch personnel into this change. Privatisation and globalisation triggered to create lot of opportunities for the banking sector. And it was upto the young leaders to exploit these opprtunities.

And that is how the age of computerisation drove home a very important point to me about re-skilling and upskilling.

Re-skilling needs an open mind. I was a science student before I came to banking. But I studied accountancy. I studied English Literature. I also pursued several certifications in banking. I did Cost Accountancy. We need to keep an open mind so as to remain relevant to what is happening in the ecosystem. If I had remained stubborn and hung on to the age-old methods of banking, I would not have been able to enjoy all the breaks that came my way. Re-skilling and upskilling helps us blend our experiences with new methods and adapt to the customer's needs. Banks too invest in training their employees and bankers need to take these opportunities seriously. To give an example: I was in Bhopal and handled many large accounts. I had some ideas on deposit mobilisation. When the Regional and Zonal Managers heard this, they suggested that I should conduct training for other branch managers on mobilising deposits at the training centre. Similarly, I had the account of Mandi Board at the Malviya Nagar branch in Bhopal. With that account, I ensured I gave them doorstep service. They would get their cheques from different areas and markets. My staff would go to their office every day, collect the cheques, prepare the schedule and give them the acknowledgement right there. I remember the then director of the company, P P Mathur who retired as the Chief Secretary of the Madhya Pradesh government, was very impressed with my banking service.

Only re-skilling is not enough, be prepared to accept change and inconvenience as well. I am a firm believer that change is the only constant. The only way to grow is to be willing to accept this change.

You need to mould yourself to whatever is required for that change, only then you can prosper. My most important message to bankers is: adopt the new technology, understand the usage of the technology and innovate on how to use it best.

One needs to accept the discomfort as well. I lived in a bungalow in Indore and travelled by car. When I was posted in Mumbai in 1994, I lived in a one bedroom house and commuted by the 8.20 a.m. train from Goregaon to Churchgate to reach office at 9.45 a.m.. Every day, I would take my scooter to the railway station and take the train from there. I would walk from the station to Nariman Point. But in just a couple of years, I was promoted to Chief Manager and I got an office car and driver as reward of my work.

It was not just me who was inconvenienced. My wife and kids had to leave every comfort they had to come to Mumbai for me. My wife would drive the kids to school and back. My family had to change houses and schools with every transfer. I have had 15 odd transfers in my career. In Mumbai alone, we have shifted five-six homes all across the city. Now I could have refused the transfers, saying that I was content to stay where I was and where my family was comfortably settled. This is very typical of bank managers in metro towns. They are very comfortable; they do not seek promotion. They are happy with what they have. But that does not give you growth. The primary requirement is that you have to compromise your comforts.

In that sense, my family has cooperated and supported me every inch of the way. They could have refused any of these changes at any given point.

Competition drives real growth. In 1991, it was the economic crisis that led to liberalisation, privatisation and globalisation. The growth and the exposure to the global world is what led our country to truly prosper. The Indian banking world, which was still very insular till then, was forced to change and re-invent itself. And it was competition that really catalysed this whole chain reaction. The emergence of private banks like UTI/Axis, ICICI, HDFC finally forced nationalised banks to take a reality check about their operations.

Competition ensures that banks keep focussing on their productivity. Private banks were computerised on day one of their operations. There is no way nationalised banks could compete in the service stakes if we continued to do all banking services manually. We had to change and adapt. When I was Regional Manager in Mumbai South, I always asked my branch managers to keep mapping the market share of our bank versus other competing banks in their areas or districts. Every banker needs to know what is their market share. If you are behind others, you need to figure how to get a better share of the market. If ahead in the stakes, you need to focus on how to remain ahead of the curve.

Personal growth happens when organisation grows. You cannot grow alone and let the organization be where it is. The growth of the individual is always linked with the organizational growth. Every manager has to strategise on where the opportunities are and how to grab them. What are those extra steps that your branch team needs to take? When I was branch manager, there was a simple exercise I would follow. I would send my team to map our area of branch operations. How many doctors are there? How many lawyers are there? How many schools are there? How many colleges are there? What are the typical businesses operating in the area? In many cities, every area is known for a particular business activity. For instance, Dadar East has many garment and saree shops while BKC has corporates and diamond businesses. Every branch manager has to know his own market and figure how his/her offering will make a difference in the market and inspire the whole team to deliver on the business goals.

In last few years, **KYC (Know Your Customer)** has gained a lot of significance in banking world. But where it comes to competition mapping, I rely on another KYC which is just as important: Know Your

Competition. There is also a KYOB exercise which I find very useful. Let me explain.

Know Your Own Bank. Every Branch and Regional Manager needs to understand their own bank and area of operations first. What are your products and services? What is your area of operation? What are the typical businesses in your area? How do they operate? What are their banking needs? We will talk in detail about this in the next chapter.

Know Your Competition. I always find it useful to walk the talk. I would walk around the streets of the locality of my branch to gain insights on the competition in that area. I would check on which banks were most visible to customers. I would check on the banners of banks or which banks were sponsoring which events, what schemes competitors were offering to their customers in a particular area. Bringing these insights to your operations will help pitch our branch into improving our own offerings.

This positive attitude also brought a lot of recognition and helped me improve my performance.

Typically Banking is considered to be a laidback profession. People tend to perceive it as a very cushy, easy-going indifferent job suited for non-ambitious people. Bankers are seen to be time-watchers and uncooperative in popular perception. But that is not true at all. Although destiny brought me to banking, I have found this industry to be extremely creative and innovative and people-centric.

Let me explain how globalisation and a few moves led to some very interesting experiences and operational learnings of the banking industry that shaped my career.

Chapter 5

The Big Shift

One of the biggest transitions in my life came after my transfer to Mumbai in 1994. After my Branch Managership in Bhopal, I came to the Siyaganj branch in 1992 in Indore. Siyaganj is a wholesale trading market of commodities. India has a big commodities export market. So I knew a lot of exporters. Indore is also a big manufacturing hub for chemicals and pharmaceuticals, which are also big on exports. So we had a separate foreign exchange desk, which was an authorised dealing branch. That was my first exposure to International Banking.

But my real learnings began when I was inducted into International Banking through invitation and selection on merit. In banking, invitations meant that the banks wanted skilled officers who could qualify for these positions. Luckily, by then, I had completed Cost Accountancy, CAIIB, and other certifications that qualified me for this position.

The phase between 1991 to 1994 was an exciting one for Indian banking. I found myself in the thick of things as the banking world unfurled in front of us. It was an economic crisis; our forex kitty was down to zero; our country had to pledge our gold with the UK and get credit against that.

The major changes that were implemented in the banking industry were on account of the Narasimhan Committee. It is extremely important to understand how this committee's recommendations impacted banking and continue to be relevant even today.

The various recommendations of this Committee have pushed banking growth through the phases of liberalisation, automation, technology and globalisation. The new generation economy also led to liberalisation of Insurance sector, formation of SEBI and other Regulatory Authorities. A lot of new societal shifts were happening in the industry, and bankers were prime witnesses to this transformation.

Transition-wise for me, this was a shift from Branch Managership to Chief Managership to a specialised Overseas branch in Mumbai. But this shift also meant leaving a town like Bhopal/Indore and coming to a big metropolis. Like I said in the earlier chapter, my family and I had to move from a spacious home in Indore to a small 1BHK in Goregaon. It meant learning to time the daily Mumbai local train at 8 am so as to reach the office by 9.30 am

But no good things happen easily. When I came to International Banking, my first task was reconciliation of NOSTRO and VOSTRO accounts, and it required a good understanding of International Banking. Our Deputy General Manager, Mr Michael Bastian, who later retired as Chairman of the Syndicate Bank, tasked me and Mr HSU Kamath, who later retired as Chairman of Vijaya Bank, with the job of reconciliation of NOSTRO accounts. A NOSTRO account refers to an account that a bank holds in a foreign currency at another bank in a foreign country. NOSTRO accounts simplify the process of exchanging and trading in foreign currencies.

All banks are supposed to maintain accounts overseas in dollar terms or pound terms or Swiss francs, or whatever currencies are accepted for global exchange. All our transactions in imports, exports, and all payments and receipts in foreign currencies get actually credited / debited to our NOSTRO accounts.

Once you get the information that your account is credited or debited, we convert foreign currency into rupees accordingly on the given exchange rate for the day and pass the entries locally. Now, whatever you are doing locally, and whatever is there in the account overseas, should be eventually reconciled. At the time, you won't believe it, there were more than three lakh outstanding entries in various NOSTRO accounts put together. This exercise wasn't easy at all. But every transaction taught us what International Banking was all about. Because before reconciliation, one had to understand the transaction itself.

If there was a credit of hundred rupees, the debit entry was for dollars equivalent to that sum. One had to understand why and how to reconcile this gap. This is how we began our study of foreign exchange transactions. Consequently, we brought down three lakh outstanding entries to three thousand. Even with the three thousand balance entries, we did a lot of interventions and enquiries. In today's world, technology helps you with such tasks. At the click of the button, you get the reconciliation statement and you can check what the outstanding entries are. If reconciliation is not done in time, some parties will lose money. In our time, we did all this manually.

Sometimes we would get calls from customers asking why their account has not been credited. We would have to reply that we could not see the credit anywhere. Now, it has improved, the technology has helped the instant reconciliation. This has helped to plug leakages and improve customer service.

My biggest lesson about foreign exchange transactions has been to look at every transaction from a complete life cycle perspective. Let's say, what you are exporting, somebody overseas is importing. Similarly, what we are importing, someone else is exporting from abroad. These are like buyer-seller transactions, but with regard to its invoicing, payment, payment realisation, they have different implications. So I would say liberalisation and globalisation expanded the vista for bankers like us, where we could help our clients expand the exports and imports business.

This stint in overseas banking also helped me understand the importance of the role of the non-resident Indian to the Indian economy. Non-resident Indians have been a treasure to Indian banking. A large number of Indians working abroad, particularly in the IT sector, are making remittances and saving huge money. Every household in the metro and urban centres has got some or other family member working overseas. Now there are branches which are dedicated only to serve Non Resident Indians for their banking requirements. But then, it was an innovative idea at that time.

In those days, there were four kinds of accounts which non-residents could have opened. One is simple NRO, which is Non-Resident Ordinary and is non-repatriable. Non-Resident External, which is repatriable, means you could convert rupee into dollars and send it back. Third is FCNR, where you put it into the foreign currency. Fourth was NRNR.

The Reserve Bank came out with a product, NRNR (Non-Resident Non-Repatriable) during 1991 crisis. This product doesn't exist today. But in this scheme, we paid an interest of 17 percent on such deposits when the country needed forex deposits badly in the early 90s. This gave me an opportunity to focus on the NRI business. I tried to find from all my customers how many family members they had residing overseas and how to connect with them. At the time, my team and I reached out to each and every family overseas and tried to convince them to start their accounts with us.

We improved our deposits by inviting the NRNR deposits, by creating more and more relationships. And once a customer comes to you for one deposit, you can offer him everything. And so that was an opportunity for us as bankers to really grow our deposit base and credit base, export import and everything.

Having concluded both projects successfully, Mr Bastian tasked me and Kamath with training the Branch Managers across the country for promoting Non-Resident deposits. This included training Managers about the types of products and services, dealing with foreign clients, canvassing for business and how to satisfy the customer and give the best services.

The other area of opportunity was to look beyond the pool of the local business people. I was heading the Union Bank Overseas branch in 1996 which was based in Opera House. Now basis my Know Your Own Bank research, the Diamond Bourse was in Opera House in those days and I realised that my area had more than a fair share of diamond traders. There were no other major businesses in the locality. My branch mainly dealt with exporters and importers. We didn't deal with savings accounts, FDs, or home loans.

So, I thought about venturing beyond diamond traders and approaching other kinds of import-export businesses. I mapped all the Export Promotion Councils in the city; there is one each for textiles, chemicals, diamonds and pharmaceuticals. I personally visited these Export Promotion Councils and collected their database of members.

I started studying this database and figured that there were listed companies and incorporated companies. To be honest, one did not get any information on incorporated companies. For the listed companies, we could take a look at the quarterly results etc. I would study those results in the financial newspapers. This gave me a lot of market and account information. I would then proactively write them a letter or mail offering our services, alongwith a request for a meeting. This unexpected move led to a lot of business for the branch.

One of those meetings led to an excellent business relationship and friendship with Mr Ganesh Gupta, who was the chairman of the local chapter of the Federation of Indian Exporters Organisation (FIEO). I met with businessmen to understand the challenges they encountered in their export-import transactions.

This phase of globalisation also opened the doors for banks to expand into international markets. That also further streamlined the services offered. Banks saw sense in expanding in the markets where the largest customer base of their clients was. Singapore, Hongkong, Antwerp were big business centres for Indian banks. This also helped Nationalised Banks to develop and improve good practices in International Banking so that we got a foothold in the Mumbai market. The Union Bank was very aggressive and advanced in International Banking business.

There was a tremendous boost that the Indian economy received because of the LPG strategy. And therefore, to sum up my learnings as a Chief Manager of Overseas branch in Mumbai:

Banking is the lifeline of an economy. An economy cannot grow by itself. In the economic parlance, credit creation has got a multiplier effect. You will ask how. Say, I give a loan to you. You use that loan to buy something. The person who sold you something bought their parts from somebody else who has engaged in labour to get something done. The complete cycle of that transaction will include labour, raw materials, manufacturing and processing. Every individual is connected in this ecosystem. Banking is the fuel. It is banking that will facilitate all these transactions, through a savings account withdrawal, loan, cheque etc.

Instead of focusing on only the business of his branch and his targets, in today's world, the banker has to understand what his contribution to society is. He should always have this larger picture before him. This must translate into his or her view about their careers as well. There are so many diplomas, courses and certifications that Managers can qualify for, which can expand their career options. There are Managers who may feel very comfortable with a Manager's position and perks, but, they have to understand that they still have 25 to 30 years to grow in their careers. They need to have a larger view of how their career can impact society.

A leader has to create leaders, not followers. The International Banking Department started in the Union Bank of India long ago. It was pioneered by the late Mr SA Kamath, who retired as Managing Director of the Bank of Maharashtra. In those days, he started this department from the Bombay Samachar Marg branch in Mumbai. He had such reach and close connection with his customers that that branch was called Kamath's bank! He had worked on that kind of image building for the bank. He was what you would call a leader's leader and inspired many of his juniors like me to excel at what we do.

As a banker, you need to succeed in team building, whether you are a Branch Manager or at the Regional or Zonal level. The important thing is to guide the team and communicate your values to them so that you can drive organisational growth together. But your people need to be part of those value systems.

A leader must create leaders. I have followed this tenet right from the beginning. In my entire career, right up to the time I became chairman, if I ever visited a branch or met a junior, I never occupied their chair. I always sat across the desk. If the branch manager is there, that is his position and chair, even if I am superior in designation. When you walk the talk, you leave the values you need to communicate. There is a lot of power in this.

Don't use a dagger when you can kill with a smile. I had the good fortune of meeting good mentors in my career. My first mentor was my Regional Manager, Mr AC Sule, when I was Branch Manager at Rewa in 1982. His philosophy was: Never use a dagger if you can kill with a smile. He used to tell us there is no point in shouting at people. One must learn to communicate their message in a manner that the person will receive it. Because unless the message is well-received, the communication is not complete. So I always communicate with a smile. That does not mean that I have never scolded anyone or faced any conflicts. But there is a way to bring up criticism respectfully.

Give yourself time to think over and understand an issue. For a Branch Manager, the most important stakeholders are the customers and the employees. Now employees get represented by unions. When union representatives come to discuss a complaint or grievance, it may be taxing for a manager to face down. At times, the grievance may also have been fabricated to instigate a superior. But the lessons I got from my mentors is that, whether right or wrong, we must listen to everybody coolly. Nothing is gained from reacting immediately. It is important to take time to understand and then react calmly. Anger only gives more weaponry to the opposite person to attack you with. Your angry comment or email will give more fodder for their grievance.

I would like to recount an episode from my managerial experience at the Rewa Siddhi Gramin Bank. There was some local political interference because of the Employee Union at that time. And somehow they wanted to instigate me against a particular Branch Manager who was not taking a decision in their favour. According to our report, he was taking the right decision as per the banking norms. But he was not taking a decision in their favour. I refused to take any decision on the matter. One day in order to pressurise me and the bank, they all came to the branch to *gherao* me with the complaint that I was not taking any action. They threatened me that they wouldn't let me step out of the branch, that my car would not be allowed to go out.

I was using a Jeep as a General Manager of Rewa Sidhi Gramin Bank, and they ensured that my Jeep was surrounded by their people. I had every opportunity to call the District Collector because I was at par with the Collector there, and I was a part of the district level consultative committee also. I also knew the Superintendent of Police in Rewa very well. But I didn't call anyone. My Branch Manager started panicking and suggested calling the collector. But I was cool. I realised that the union representatives had grievances. I asked them to wait for half an hour so that I could understand the matter from my manager. I asked them to have tea while they waited. Once I was clear on the stand of my Branch Manager, I met them calmly and explained to them how wrong their demand was. I assured them that the bank was working for the welfare of the employees as well as the Sidhi district residents. I talked to them for 2–3 hours but finally they were mollified.

And that is how I returned home. In hindsight, I realise, had I reacted angrily, it would have unnecessarily aggravated the whole situation. As a leader, I believe that it is better to resolve a situation rather than let it aggravate.

There are times when a manager feels like saying 'Get Lost' to a customer or an employee. But he is saying those words in anger; he doesn't really want the customer or employee to leave the bank. But when you say those words aloud, things will flare up. There have been instances when I have lost my cool or gotten annoyed. But then once I cooled down, I would go and apologise.

Things get flared up. My advice to young bankers would be to always keep your cool with the most important constituents of your life: your employees, customers, bosses and family as well. You will never regret it.

Some day or the other, every banker encounters a difficult situation where he may utter something that he never intended to. And that leads to a complicated situation because, all said and done, the banking industry totally depends on human behaviour.

Know the strengths of your branch and your team. It is important for Managers to understand their own strengths. I would like to give an example. I was a Branch Manager in Arera Colony branch in 1990. A week after I joined the branch, I got a telegraphic transfer in the name of EPCO, that is Environmental Pollution Control Board. This transfer was from Ministry of Environment in Delhi. Typically, when the money transfer comes, we prepare the credit check for them and then deliver it to them. I thought this was a great opportunity. I was aware that the Union Bank of India was the official banker for Ministry of Environment and Forest at the central level.

I immediately picked up that wire transfer and went to their office, which was nearby. I asked to meet their senior officials. I explained to them that the Union Bank was their parent banker at the corporate office level, and it was most desirable if they were to start an account with me. I told them that if they started banking with us, they would get immediate credit as opposed to the present situation where they had to wait for two days for the amount to clear. So that was the driving point. They were convinced, and they opened an account with us the very next day. I drove a lot of Institutional business for the branch, only on the basis of its strategic location and the business around it.

Create awareness in your client base. When you have understood clearly what the strengths of your team and your branch are, your next duty is to let your clients know what you are offering. To accomplish this, it is important to communicate with your customers or target audience. If you meet them at the branch, take the time to talk to your customers and ask them questions. Talk to their kids or parents who have accompanied them to the branch. Ask about the family whenever you meet a customer. Offer to open a kids' account for them or discuss fixed or recurring deposits for them. If you have an insurance product to sell, you have to inform every customer that you have the scheme. When we embarked on the Suraksha Bima Yojana, we would ask every customer if their drivers, personal staff, or maids had taken the Bima scheme. We would also explain why it is important to insure your staff.

If you are sponsoring a cultural event, it is not enough to just have a banner and an announcement for your branch. Ensure that there is a stall and that your bank representatives are talking to prospective customers at the event. Ensure that you are reaching the last mile of your customer's family. And that was simply how we got business. So awareness and approach—these are the buzzwords for any banker to always bear in mind.

Credit should be by choice and not by chance. As Chief Manager of the Overseas Branch, I was very clear that if I wished to grow our business, I must have all the information about my customers available. Even after I approached the Export Promotion Council and got their database, I went through each and every company and looked at their information before approaching them. This approach helped us in two ways. First, we understood what the customer's needs are. Second, in our quest to win business, we must not end up with unsavoury clients.

A manager has to make a conscious decision that he will lend by his choice. He or she has to determine that a borrower has potential so that both the bank and client can benefit. I will elaborate on this further in the credit risk management chapters ahead.

Don't put all your eggs in one basket. Like I said, my overseas branch was based in Opera House, Mumbai, and the area had the diamond bourse. Most of our clients were diamond traders. But I decided that I will also focus on important sectors other than the diamond business. In the initial months itself, I had researched 5–6 sectors which I had identified as a potential growth sector for Indian exports. And that is what I chose to focus on growing.

After the rough, comes the smooth. To sum up, it is important to understand that although liberalisation, privatisation and globalisation came on the heels of a very rough time in banking, they led to immense benefits for the banking industry as well as the customer. The Reserve Bank and the Finance Minister at the time had a long-term view. Today, we can see the benefits of that view. We are the fifth largest economy, and we are trying to become the third largest by 2047.

In banking, this long-term approach yields many benefits. We need to draw a road map on the basis of this view. Operationally, one of the most important factors for this long term growth was core banking. This technology enabled data analysis and transaction banking forever changed banking in India. I will be discussing these in the next chapter.

Chapter 6

The Revolution: Core Banking and its Impact

Although the process of computerisation began in 1988, it took a long time for computerisation to take hold and be practised operationally in the industry. In case of the Union Bank of India, we started the process in 1988. We went phase by phase with branch automation under Core Banking which began in 2002. But 100 percent automation, which included core banking, was only achieved in 2007. By then, we had 4000 plus branches. 100 percent automation meant operational as well as delivery of customer-facing services. When the first few of our first branches were initiated into Core Banking, I was posted as Senior Manager at the Industrial Finance branch in Mumbai. I had the privilege of escorting Mr Anand Mahindra along with our Chairman, Mr Leeladhar, to our branch for the inauguration. Through my personal experience, I can say that Core Banking technology tremendously improved efficiency and productivity in banking, seeing the kind of learnings and impact we received when all our branches got hooked up to a central hub. It brought about sea change, not only in our operations, but also our approach to customer-centricity.

The biggest advantage of core banking was that the customer was no longer a customer for only the branch; he became the customer of the bank itself. One of the first applications of the technology in the banking industry, where the complete balance sheet preparation, which was again a tiresome job, was taken care of by technology. And as each branch prepared its balance sheet, it would send the numbers to their controlling office. These days, the balance sheet is all printed from the computers, it gets consolidated automatically, and even the auditing is done online. In fact in the era of COVID, complete auditing of the balance sheet has happened virtually. The auditors did not have to go physically to the banks' branches, but they managed to do it virtually.

The biggest challenge for core banking solutions was with the Mumbai zone. All my branches were very big in size and volume of business, and the transition from standalone branch to total branch automation to Core Banking was full of challenges. Once 100 percent Core Banking had been achieved, it meant that our entire bank was connected with one single solution.

With the entire data of the bank located centrally, we had access to unlimited information on what our branch numbers were, who our customers were, how they were spending their money, what products and services would be suitable to them. I reaped the benefit of this data for all our business plan strategies for the bank as a whole when I was Deputy General Manager Planning. With Core Banking at our disposal, I realised we could consider the bottom-up approach in planning rather than top-down.

The top-down approach is very simple. You just issue the growth numbers to the field and strictly monitor that they stick to their target numbers. The head decides in advance what kind of growth they are looking for in deposits, credit and so on. But we didn't work that way. We gave indicative numbers top-down. But we wanted regional offices to recommend their own growth strategy from the branches.

When you are a Regional Manager, there will be number of branches reporting to you. Some of these could be rural, urban, semi-urban and metro branches. You cannot expect uniform percentage growth in all branches.

And thus every Regional Manager and Zonal Manager today has to map the potential of growth for each of his/her branches and accordingly issue business targets. To do this, it is important to understand the strengths of each of your branches. If it is a branch in a residential colony, it will be a deposit-oriented branch. If you give them credit target, it won't work. But you can give them a higher deposit target, because that is achievable.

A residential area has great potential for deposit growth. This kind of approach was possible only and only because of the technology which made all the numbers available to us from our central hub.

Because of Core Banking, we had district-wise, state-wise and zone-wise numbers. We realised that we needed a differentiated approach to the market and clients to drive business growth for our bank. With this thought in mind, our Chairman Mr MV Nair conceived the set-up of a Transaction Banking department for the Union Bank of India.

Every transaction is a new customer. When a customer transitions from being catered to by the branch to being catered by the bank itself, it means the bank's entire might and knowhow has to be geared to serve that customer. I was tasked with the job of studying the global best practices to leverage on technology and offer customised technology backed solutions to corporate institutions and individuals and other segments of the clientele of a bank. To do this, we had partnered with the Boston Consulting Group, with whom I was supposed to work very closely in order to conceive how the Transaction Banking department would work.

After much research and strategic thinking, we zeroed down on creating five sub-verticals under this department. These sub-verticals were: Cash Management, Currency Management, Payment and Settlements, distribution of Third -Party Products like, Insurance, Mutual Funds, etc, Trade Finance and Government Business. I had to choose the leaders for heading all these five sub-verticals and I was supposed to guide these leaders to achieve their targets.

Besides this, I was also given the target of identifying 500 new centres for branch expansion under the transaction banking department. This was to adhere to the basic fundamental principle already initiated by the Reserve Bank of India which was Inclusive Growth. When you talk of inclusive growth by various initiatives under the aegis of financial inclusion, every bank was expected to identify unbanked and Under-Served areas and decide to have the presence in that geographical pocket. But when you work on a branch expansion, it is not mere presence which is the determinant. It is the viability of that unit which is the most important part. That if I set up a branch there which will have a fixed infrastructure, which will have the manpower, there will be a fixed cost to run that. Now in order to make that unit viable, you have to work on the business potential.

So we got into the SWOT (Strengths, Weakness, Opportunities, Threats) analysis of the branch's operational areas, we did the environmental scanning and concluded a proper assessment of all these centres before we applied to the RBI. Within nine to 12 months we got approval for all 500 branches,. We opened 196 branches and 644 new ATMs with this feasibility study.

One of those branches was a branch with a customer lobby at Banjara Hills in Hyderabad. We had actually done the virtual inauguration of the branch through the hands of the then Finance Minister P Chidambaram. This was in 2008.

In transaction banking, visibility is everything. During my career, nothing widened my perspective about banking more than when I was associated with the re-branding activities of the Union Bank of India. After initiating transaction banking and all its services, Mr Nair decided that the logo and corporate personality of the Union Bank of India needed to undergo a change as well. He launched a programme called Navniram which would reflect what our bank had come to stand for after the introduction of Core Banking and Transaction Banking. Every public sector bank has a different character and a different method of driving its businesses. But interestingly, lot of my research suggested that, for the masses, all public sector banks look the same. Most of them thought that public sector banks were government owned and were all similar in their approach to customer service.

The Union Bank of India needed its own identity to represent the change we were undergoing in our approach to customer service and technology. The logo was about 25 years old. It didn't make any impact on the new generation at all. Computers and Internet had come in and the role of banking had drastically changed. Customer-centricity had become key. A new logo, that reflected all these features, had to be conceptualised.

So we created a new logo, the letter of U of the Union Bank interlinked with a reverse U to denote 'you,' meaning the customer, to depict that the Union Bank Is For You. The colour scheme was blue and red to convey that the Union Bank was vibrant, cool and agile. And after a lot of internal and external research we campaigned the logo change saying, "Your dreams are not yours alone."

In the process of changing our colour scheme, our logo, I got a firsthand experience of viewing the brand of the Union Bank of India objectively, and then assess it against dozen of banks and their branding. It helped me understand how to define what a bank brand should stand for and what qualities it needs to portray. We decided to continue and practice our tagline " Good people to bank with."

To be honest, more branches also meant more visibility for the bank. Each branch and ATM becomes a source of publicity for the bank. Conscious of this, we spent lot of time on creating the creative standards, standard look and feel of the Branches, the ATM, and the Services. This way, the customer gets a standard visual and emotional feel in all branches and

ATMs of the Union Bank of India. So on that fundamental, we worked and opened these many units, which definitely helped us in creating the brand image of the bank.

It is important to mention that when a bank is developing these kind of services, it is important to research in detail the global best practices. The second factor is to understand what your customer segment expects from you.

I would like to talk about one incident here. In 1998, I had travelled to San Francisco to attend an Executive Development Programme convened by the Bank Of America for global representatives in banking. I remember visiting a branch of the Wells Fargo Bank which actually had a coffee shop and laundry! I was quite perplexed, and I remember asking their team lead why they had designed a bank branch with a coffee shop and laundry in it.

Their answer was that they had a lot of youngsters as customers. These youngsters often lived alone and did not have a pantry or laundry equipment in their homes. They designed this branch in a way that youngsters multi-tasked even as they were banking. This way, the young customer would always value their bank over others. I was impressed with this thought! What a thought, that too as early as 1998. That incident stayed with me. Transaction Banking needs that level of customer-centric thinking where service offerings are concerned.

Now, we cannot have a bank branch with a coffee shop or a laundry in India. But this incident guided me when we were planning branch expansion and amenities to be provided to customers within the Branches

In today's age, it is therefore extremely important to keep the busy new millennial on your horizon, think about how they will perceive your services. Keeping those things in mind, we developed a self-service lobby that would attract Internet savvy youngsters to avail our services without delay.

In a self-service customer lobby, apart from basic ATM services of cash withdrawal, what are the other services that should be available? There should be an enquiry counter, account enquiry portal, a cash deposit machine, an automated cheque deposit service, passbook printing and so on. We took care to build all those features into the customer experience. This branch infrastructure helped our Transaction Banking services. We had built this department on five pillars. I will briefly describe each and how they impacted our bank's growth.

1. Cash Management Service

2. Currency Chest

3. Payments & Settlements

4. Marketing Of Third Rarty products

5. Government Business & Trade Finance

Cash Management Services

This is a very important institutional service. I am giving a small example of a Non-Banking Finance Company. In those days, NBFC lenders would collect post-dated cheques for instalments. If an NBFC has a 1000 customers, and they take 36 cheques for 3 years, they are dealing with a large amount of cheques which they have to deposit in their bank with respect to different accounts on different dates. This is a very cumbersome process. So we offered a service that you deposit all these cheques with my bank and I will log these cheques from cash management department. It means I am fronting all their monthly activity. So we would collect all these cheques, keep them in storage and create a database so that every month we deposit 1000 cheques with different EMI dates.

This concept was borrowed from the Corporation Bank, which had initiated the cash management service first. Eventually, the bank itself got merged with the Union Bank. For this project, we hired an experienced person in cash management. My main role was to reach out to corporates with this product and convince them to try out cash management at our bank. We had to show them that this product would reduce their hassles of banking and help their operations immensely. They did not need a person specifically to go to the bank and deposit cheques everyday. As for the bank, we got paid for the transaction or handling of every instrument. It was a great revenue model. Companies didn't mind paying us for this service. This service was very successful; we were able to successfully sort their recurring receipts and payments. We also got the benefit of deposits in their current accounts.

We started this service from a small back office room hooked up to the central hub. We created good volumes, so the profit generation was not a challenge. The other advantage of cash management was that it helped us in reaching to the various corporate institutions where we did not have an institutional relationship.

Research the Institution Carefully. The way to build an institutional relationship is to study the Organisation before you reach the Organisation. Then you work out what you can offer that will complement and ease the work of that organisation and improve its productivity. These relationships can be cultivated and built only when you are in a position to improve the functioning of the organisation. That is how collaborations can happen and synergies can be leveraged.

I would like to recall one incident in HPCL. I proposed to HPCL that they should avail of our cash management services. But they replied that all their payments were captured in their ERP process and that was connected to one multinational bank. At the end of the day, the accounts department forwards this file to that bank. With such meetings with large institutions I also learned that some banks were way ahead of us in offering best services.

That got us started on working out whether we could develop a sort of a middleware, what we call it in technology language, which could connect the technology of the Institution and the Bank together. Because from the cybersecurity perspective, you cannot link any infrastructure to your core banking infrastructure directly. It has to go through the middleware.

Currency Chest

This was another interesting initiative we started in the Union Bank. Typically in every bank, the currency chest is a place where all the excess cash in the branches is deposited. Whatever deposits of excess cash you make there, gets credited to your current account with the Reserve Bank of India. Currency chest service is basically management of cash on behalf of the Reserve Bank of India. So, you get the immediate credit and debits for whatever transactions happen during the day. In those days, the currency chest division was always seen to be a cost centre. No one had really thought about monetising this rich asset of cash.

One way to look at it was that every branch has to have sorted cash. When banks were embarking on the expansion of the ATMs, those machines needed sorted cash. Then only can the ATMs be fit. So, the primary requirement is high-end technology-driven machineries for sorting purposes. So, we thought of that solution. We researched the market and figured that the counting machines were there. Counting by hand was prone to errors and mismanagement. So we ensured counting machines in every Currency Chest in the Union Bank. Then we focussed on employees in various branches or fields who were not comfortable with customer-facing jobs. We trained these resources in currency chest management and also set standard operating procedures, right from uniforms to software and so on. We also spoke about how this division could really contribute to the organisation's growth.

There was considerable risk since it was the handling of cash after all. So we introduced the proper checks and balances, security measures, alarms, cameras. We had already worked on the projections on what the income would be against the costs. We started selling sorted cash to various banks that did not have the requisite facilities but had ATMs.

Many private sector banks had a huge network of ATMs vis-a-vis public sector, but they didn't have that much of cash avenues for deployment. So, we started selling sorted cash to them and earned service charges out of that. We also started doing price transfers. Typically, the currency chest would be connected to a certain branch. And that branch would be saddled with the cost. With the currency chest division, there was a separate unit created where the cost was getting controlled and also then allocated to all the branches which took advantage of this service. This way, every branch was sending cash to the currency chest as per their convenience.

We introduced an efficient collection and delivery mechanism where no branch had to depute any staff from their branches. The cash would be collected from their branches in closed boxes with all details. And cash would be delivered to them in a similar fashion. We engaged service agencies who would pick up the cash. A service agency was allocated an area of 4–5 branches which they would visit to pick up and deliver cash after business hours.

This solved a huge problem for the bank. At that time, every branch used to hold more cash than necessary, only in expectation that they may have to make a big payment in near future. But if, as a Branch Manager, I am calculating my cash needs in the right manner as per my branch cash holding limits, the Branch didn't need to keep so much cash handy. If there is a certainty that they will get cash in 24 hours, the branch need not to hold the cash unnecessarily over the limit.

Having said that, we managed to move Rs 100 crore of cash from branches to the currency chest. In those days, we used to get 4 percent interest on the cash in hand in the currency chest in order to maintain the cash reserve ratio. Now 4 percent on Rs 100 crore in itself is Rs 4 crore. That became the income of the currency chest.

Our bank was the first to have modernised this whole division and turned it into a profit centre.

Payments And Settlement

This was the third vertical created. It covers alternate delivery channels like ATMs, debit cards, credit cards, internet banking, mobile banking, and various products for payment and settlement, which could be salary or EMI products and so on. This vertical facilitated the complete range of services for Payments & Settlements.

For each of these activities, I had to ensure that we created the necessary infrastructure. The very first was creating the proper infrastructure for 644 ATMs in the country. I had the honour of getting the 1000th ATM inaugurated in Banjara Hills, Hyderabad, which was designed with a customer lobby at that time. Setting up one ATM starts with locating the place, engaging the machinery, connecting the machinery to the technology and getting into the cash management relationship, because you need the people to manage the cash at the ATMs and then the agencies, who will connect technology in the back office to get connected to the ATM.

I had to drive all these initiatives taking the support of my technology department. But the larger objective of the payment and settlement department was to figure if we can increase the digital transactions in the branch vis-a-vis the existing digital transactions.

Think Out Of The Box

With this objective in mind, the Union Bank of India launched prepaid cards a little before Diwali of 2008. These cards could be basically loaded with a specific amount of money and could be swiped like a credit card. I remember promoting these prepaid cards in innovative ways. Typically, during Diwali you see a lot of companies, factories disburse bonuses or exgratia payments to their employees in cash. The problem is that the cash does not reach the home at all. It all gets spent in gambling or alcohol. Our whole intent was to figure out how this money could be used for the benefit of family members during the festival. We convinced our client companies to disburse their bonus cash payments through prepaid cards customised for the employees. These cards could be used at the ATM for withdrawing cash or on the card machine when making any purchases. Later, we used the idea of prepaid cards to distribute scholarships to students on behalf of the Chhatisgarh government. Usually it was found that it was parents who used the scholarship money given as cash for their household expenses. The whole purpose of a scholarship is that it should be used on educational expenses like books or tuition. Our initiative to distribute scholarships through prepaid cards was also extremely successful. In the Central Bank of India, we took the prepaid card initiative a step further with the CentYatra concept. These were basically cards loaded with foreign currency to be used while travelling abroad. Banks are authorised by the Reserve Bank of India to disburse foreign currency as per the eligibility under the FEMA guidelines.

Initially, all of us used to carry either currency or traveler's cheques, but that could be stolen. And everyone did not have an international credit card or debit card. But anybody could get an international prepaid card. Besides, this prepaid card was interoperable: even if you had loaded it with US dollars for your first trip, you could pay for something with Euros on your next trip. I still use prepaid dollar cards for my foreign travels. It was a great idea.

Innovations happen when we look at what is required to solve a customer's problems. Young leaders in banking should look at what are the persisting problems in the system that they would like to address. It is these solutions that can be converted into opportunities.

I would say that our need to reduce the physical cash withdrawals, deposits and all the cash handling issues surrounding them led to great opportunities for banks to offer cashless products. Similarly, persisting issues with cheque clearing and payments have helped customers migrate to digital transactions.

Marketing Of Third Party Products

The fourth vertical, which I would like to mention, which is extremely important for the banking industry, is marketing of third-party products, which are Insurance, Wealth Management, such as Mutual fund and Pension schemes. These three products provide protection and financial security to the society at large.

As Deputy General Manager, I was in charge of marketing for this department. In 2004, the penetration of insurance, mutual funds or pension in our society was very low. I would say that it is very low even today, but it is gradually increasing. The Union Bank was the first to tie up with HDFC Standard Life to distribute their insurance products.

Now we had tried marketing these products in 2004. But it had not taken off at the time. But in 2008, we tried this differently through the transaction banking department. In transaction banking, it is extremely essential to understand that you are not only selling an insurance product, but you are actually caring for your customers. That is the objective. When you say you're caring for a customer and that is the objective, then you make proper enquiries through the marketing team and the front office in the branches and then match their capacity to offer an insurance product towards protection and saving.

Insurance as a product is not only about protection or about saving. It is a mix of both. Taking that into view, for each branch we tried to work out a plan to identify potential customers. The marketing was done in a very focussed manner. Those efforts paid good dividends in expanding our insurance business in such a way, that the sizeable business we earned prompted the Union Bank of India to have its own subsidiary for insurance by 2008. We also launched the Star Union Daichi Insurance and became a part of the insurance company driven as a subsidiary. This was possible only because we had a capability to reach to our customer and to understand his needs and make an offering that matched his requirements.

Insurance Selling Needs Rigorous And Regular Training

As a part of the launch of our insurance offerings, I had to ensure that I trained our teams regularly on the new developments and products in the insurance industry. Insurance has several products, all of which need to be understood well before offering them to a customer. The right insurance product will tremendously enrich a customer's life, while the wrong product will be a loss to him. This is important to know because sellers get good commissions on insurance as a product. So there is always a possibility that a salesperson may offer the wrong product to customer just to earn a high commission. This kind of misselling gives a bad name to the bank too.

The good thing was that the Insurance Regulatory and Development Authority of India (IRDAI) had introduced a certification test for every marketing officer to be able to sell insurance. So that was most important but we also ensured that in our vertical, constant training was imparted to the marketing team so that they did not get in the wrong marketing of the products.

The other product that we embarked on was mutual fund distribution. With insurance, banks were allowed to sell products of only one company as a corporate agent. But in mutual funds, it was an open infrastructure, and thus all mutual funds were approaching banks. We were supposed to understand the products of all mutual funds so as to best offer what the customer needed.

There was another reason that required constant training and updation. On one level, there were existing customers who were already investing in mutual funds. But there was one constraint Branch Managers faced with selling mutual funds. If the manager is asked to sell mutual fund products, the customer may divert his deposit towards the wealth management product. And to that extent, his deposit level comes down. So there was some reluctance to sell these products to customers. We had to do a lot of training to make managers understand that they could not stop customers from investing in any wealth management products and that they could understand the behaviour of the customers through the operations in their account and accordingly tap them for wealth management products.

This is another place where core banking technology helped us. It was data on the banking operations which core banking threw up that helped us with customer identification. By only looking at the operations of the account, we could identify customers who were suitable for mutual fund investments. And that really helped managers offer these products better. As a result, our income from insurance and mutual fund products grew by almost 40 percent to 50 percent in those years. Therefore, like insurance, the bank considered starting its own subsidiary for distribution for mutual funds as well. The Union Bank of India again tied up with a Belgium company called KBC to roll a subsidiary in 2009.

Both these subsidiaries of insurance and mutual fund got rolled out after I moved out of the Union Bank of India. But it was a tremendous base we created right from 2002. The most important part for any leader at the level of top management in the banking industry is that you have to ensure that even in future your organisation gets the benefit of your hard work. I'm very happy that even today both the subsidiaries are operational in the insurance and mutual fund industry.

Another product we marketed was the National Pension Scheme. So the Pension Fund Regulatory Development Authority (PFRDA) came up with this new product; earlier pension was either available to government employees or bankers. Some of the public sector undertakings also did not have pension benefits and would opt for LIC pension products. So the pension penetration in our society was extremely low. This was one area of opportunity which PFRDA identified instantly. I had the opportunity to attend a few PFRDA meetings as General Manager of the Union Bank of India during the launch of NPS. This was another product which we embarked on marketing, identifying customers, particularly from institutions where their services are not pensionable, and who had some capability to save. This also proved a very successful effort since there was a real need for customers to save for their pensions.

Another product which came as a new product in the banking industry was from the capital markets, which was called ASBA. ASBA means Application Supported by Blocked Amount. This account has authorisation to block application money in the bank account when a customer is subscribing to an issue. It was a great product to promote retail investors in the capital market. Because in the good old days before ASBA, customers were supposed to give a cheque. Now the cheque would have to be deposited and would remain with the organisation for 45 days. Until a complete allocation was made, the customer would not get a refund, and his or her money would be stuck.

This innovation allowed retail investors to block this amount in their savings accounts itself. When this was launched by SEBI in 2008, my Chairman, Mr MV Nair, gave me a challenge to ensure that our bank should be the first bank to tie up with SEBI on ASBA, and we achieved it.

The most important learning from this department was how to convert an opportunity into a business. And it was the technology that brought about these opportunities. Today, we are all talking about digitisation, digital marketing and all that. But our bank had a very futuristic view in identifying these necessities. The moment we have a product that fits the customer's needs and the technology to fulfil that need, it is a win-win situation. ASBA accounts helped us identify customers who were interested in capital markets, and we could help them transact without disturbing their savings accounts.

We were already offering demat accounts and trading facilities in conjunction with the brokers on an online trading platform. This way we could bundle our services together where a savings bank with the Union Bank would also offer an ASBA account, demat services on an online trading platform. These marketing tools helped expand our savings bank account portfolio.

In today's competitive market, every customer should have a good reason to continue with your bank as a preferred bank.

Government Business And Trade Finance

This was the last vertical under transaction banking. In government circles, typically certain banks are allocated to certain ministries as parent bank. The Union Bank of India was a principal banker for the Ministry of Environment and Forest. Now that is an opportunity. How does one leverage on this situation? When you want to canvas institutional business from a big client like a Ministry, you should have something special to offer that client so that their budget allocation fund which they draw for spending, initially remains with the Bank. And towards that, we had set up a Government Business Cell.

For this we had devised a three-pronged approach. First, we tried to procure the pension accounts of the various public sectors where pension processing is done. There is a great opportunity in driving the pension accounts of the public sector undertakings.

Because if you are approaching any public sector undertaking, and you are their banker for pension distribution approved by the state governments, the employees choose your bank and park the pension funds they get on retirement as provident fund or gratuity and that deposit comes to you. So we started moving on to approach different government departments. I would like to recap a couple of points here.

Proactive efforts pay dividends over the long term. In 2007–8, the government of India had come out with the urbanization programme under the JNNURM, that is Jawaharlal Nehru National Urban Renewal Mission. Under the programme, it was envisaged that a lot of activities will be driven by the local municipal corporations who would raise funds through the bonds. They would have a credit rating and embark on the various activities of waste management, infrastructure development, transport and so on for the Municipal Corporations.

The moment this programme was declared, we approached the state government and offered to drive these activities for the government in a few states where we had good presence. We were the Lead Bank in Madhya Pradesh and Uttar Pradesh in a couple of districts and also had good presence in Gujarat. So we started connecting with Municipal Corporations in those states and started working on their programmes on waste management and began funding these initiatives.

Keep an eye on your ecosystem. The point of bringing up all these issues is that if you are keeping an eye on what is happening in the system around you, it can be beneficial for the business. I'll give a small example. The government has recently announced the 100 smart city programmes. This is a great opportunity for a present day banker to get in touch with those districts, if they are the Lead Bank of that district, and plan for business opportunities.

A bank could be one of the co-promoters of the smart cities by engaging with the government or private agencies who would want to come and set up there. They could finance the new projects which are coming up and become a part of the growth of the smart city. This is what we did with government business and trade finance.

Basically trade finance means the import and export business or the businesses which are happening through the letter of credits and bank guarantees. Now, here I'll give a couple of examples.

In 2002, The Union Bank of India launched Depository Services in the bank through Mumbai Samachar Marg branch. We had our branch located just opposite Bombay Stock Exchange, and we had a good number of current accounts of brokers who operated there, but we realised that the brokers did not patronise us to issue bank guarantees for margin funding and various activities in favor of Bombay Stock Exchange.

So we set up a separate Capital Market Cell in that branch during my tenure. We leveraged on this and issued the bank guarantees of almost Rs 500 crore, which helped us in getting a deposit of Rs 250 crore with a 50 percent cash deposit margin, and earned commissions for the bank. Armed with my experience with the BS Marg branch, we decided to try and make trade finance convenient for the customers to do business with us. So keeping an eye out for existing opportunities is very important.

Focus on Customer Relationship Management (CRM). This is very important. For instance, we were already selling life insurance. We already had the infrastructure. Now if there is some opportunity to sell non-life insurance or general insurance, we should explore that too. Every customer who comes to a bank may have a scooter or a car. Is that insured? Could you sell them an insurance policy? All your customers have homes. Could you sell them household theft or breakdown policy? As a banker, one needs to know how best to cater to this. If someone is coming to you for a home or car loan, recommend that they insure the home or the car for their benefit. To do this, we created a team in each branch headed by a trained marketing officer certified by the IRDAI. Although it is difficult to sell all products to all customers, bankers must look at those opportunities. Whatever lending we do is done to create an asset. That asset needs to be covered and the borrower also needs to be covered. For instance, when a person takes a home loan, the borrower and the asset both need to be covered, otherwise the loan repayment will get impacted in the event of death of borrower. This is not only to protect the loan repayment but also the family of the borrower who will be saddled with his or her long term debt. Therefore, it is the banker's duty to recommend term insurance for the borrower and property insurance for the home to protect both parties.

There is a huge potential for insurance penetration in India and banks are best placed to promote this cause in the market. For this purpose, CRM gives you a 360 degree view of a customer and his or her needs.

I will take you back to my 1998 experience of visiting the Well Fargo bank in San Francisco, which had a laundry and coffee shop. When I was the Zonal Manager for the Mumbai zone, we opened retail outlets for housing loans. In each of those outlets, apart from the housing loan itself, we gave them information about all the projects coming up in different areas of Mumbai. If there was a branch in Goregaon, then that branch would have the details of all the projects right from Bandra to Mira Road. Now the customer knows that his bank is giving him multiple pre-approved property choices along with the home loan as well. Once he takes the loan, I could offer to insure his house as well, all under one roof. So although I was unable to open the laundry and coffee shop at the branch, I was able to adapt that same customer-centric idea to another setting.

Offline time counts. This finally brings me to the role of footfall in a branch. As bankers, we always wanted to encourage footfall to our branches. The idea of creating a customer lobby was to encourage customers to visit for a hassle-free experience, so we had all these gadgets and service pods in place so that physical footfalls at the branches could be converted into the lobby. A customer's visit to the branch is an incredible opportunity to engage with him or her. But in regular banking, customers may find that branch is crowded and so there may hardly be any interaction that happens between the front office and the customer.

Then how do you get a 360-degree view of the customer? There needs to be interaction with the customer to understand the needs of the customer and pitch the products that can really suit him. In order to do all this, you need sufficient time in the branches. But if your front office staff is busy only doing transactional activity of cash withdrawals or check deposits or a passbook printing, what do you do?

Now this is where the idea of the customer lobby comes in. In specialised branches, we shifted out the transactional services of the branch and created a more presentable lobby, which was run by a customer relationship officer who would engage patiently with the client. This reduces a lot of burden on the front office staff, and that time can be used for more productive activities. This pleasant experience can bring about a lot of conversions in business.

However, in today's world, the most efficient banks are the ones where the customer doesn't have to come to the branch at all. In the era of digitisation, customers find it tiresome to go to the branch. Then how do you engage with him or her? Encourage your customer to visit your website or app and give him or her great service on it. Customer convenience will ensure more engagement for your bank. Whether on an app, website, or in person, it is only engagement that impresses customers, and the important thing for bankers is to create more opportunities and conducive infrastructure for this to happen.

And all this was possible because of core banking technology. In a nutshell, it allows bankers to get a larger business perspective of what their business operations are. I always told my juniors that Branch Managers have to believe like they are CEOs of their respective branches or departments; they need to understand all the aspects of their business and have a better understanding of what banking is. Let me outline in detail in the coming chapter.

Chapter 7

Think Like a CEO

When I say think like a CEO, what do I mean? Several things. But mainly, if you are serious about a career in banking, it is important to have a bird's eye view of what banking is.

Till you are a General Manager, you are responsible and answerable for only the vertical or zone that you represent. But as you progress in your career, your horizons have to expand. Your perspective has to encompass all the businesses of the bank.

And this perspective doesn't come with career progress. I would say that career progression happens because of this perspective.

To begin with, a manager has to look at his department's operations in terms of profitability and additional sources of income. When Transaction Banking was kicked off, it enabled banks to optimise other income as well. In private sector banks, other income as a percentage of total income has been high from the very beginning. They could focus on this because their client base was niche. Whereas in a public sector bank, while the client base is very diverse, the cut-throat focus on income is not present.

Transaction Banking gave a new lease of life to public sector banking. It allowed a public sector bank like the Union Bank of India to increase its income from all services. Besides, Core Banking allows a customer to transact directly with the bank rather than with the branch as the only interface. And therefore, it became imperative for Branch Managers, to change their perspective; managers had to start thinking of their branch as an independent business unit and think of themselves as the CEO of that business unit.

When one is thinking like a CEO, they should first look at building the balance sheet of the branch or department in the right manner.

Pay close attention to your costs. This is what makes the difference. Transaction Banking was one way to leverage the potential and resources of the branch. In the banking industry, there is a parameter called cost-to-income ratio. This particular efficiency ratio needs to be understood by all the bankers.

It is basically the operating cost divided by net interest income plus non-interest income. The lower the cost-to-income ratio of your bank or vertical, the better the efficiency. The ideal ratio is 40 percent. If you want to bring this ratio down, there are two ways to do it.

You could reduce the numerator, that is the operating cost, or improve the denominator, which is the net-interest income plus non-interest income. Now how do you look at these two parameters? Let us talk about the Operating Costs. Operating costs comprise of employee cost plus other costs. No employee would like the employee cost to be reduced. One would like increments to be released and pay hikes to be given. So operating costs never get reduced, since typically employee cost is almost 70 percent plus of the total operating cost.

Thus, there is hardly any chance to reduce the numerator. Other variable costs, paper costs, printing cost, telephone cost, etc can be reduced and optimised, but only to an extent. But there is a big value in improving your denominator, that is the net interest income and the non-interest income.

What is a net interest income? Net interest income is the difference in yield on advances and cost of deposit. Now it is the prudent mix of the assets, that is all kinds of advances, which maximises the yield on advances.

Now, if you look at retail and corporate lending, retail typically gives me better earnings. Second is the non-interest income. What is a non-interest income? It is a fee income which you earn from various services. In today's time, the fee income largely comes from the distribution of third party products like insurance distribution, mutual fund distribution, pension product distribution, etc. Additionally, you are servicing on the Trade Finance, that is the Letter of Credit, Bank Guarantees and all those services. It also includes service charges for various lending activities, like retail loans, housing loans, car loans etc. This is a concept of the cost-to-income ratio as explained in the earlier paragraph. Here you have a responsibility to bring down the operating cost which is the numerator, and upscale the denominator which is a non-interest income plus net interest income._That will bring a very qualitative Build up of the balance sheet.

This is at the Branch Manager level. But when we talk about the CMD level, he is only an aggregator of the information and the statistics generated by 4,000 CEOs operating at the branch level. And as a CEO, you have to understand the implications of both the liability and asset side of the balance sheet. Here, non-performing assets also have a role to play. NPAs have a dual impact; the bank loses interest income as well as needs to provide for probable loss.

There are efficiency and productivity parameters in the bank. Productivity is measured by the business per employee, profit per employee. Efficiency is measured by the various efficiency parameters, like what is the Return on Equity, Return on Assets, Return on Investment, Net Interest Margin, or what is the CASA percentage, so on and so forth.

From the early days as Regional Manager, I ensured that all my reportees follow and adopt these practices of improving productivity as discussed in all Business Plan meetings. This impacted our efforts on business expansion very positively.

Post retirement I also conducted 25 to 30 Executive Development Programmes for the Banking Industry on a strategic approach to improve productivity and efficiency in banks by the Senior Executives.

Know your market. The first step as CEO of a branch is to understand the market one operates in. For a bank branch, that would mean a 5-10km radius around you. I have always asked my Branch Managers to create a diary and share what is the potential business available in their area of operation. At times, this included doing the rounds of all areas in the neighbourhood and noting down: How many doctors, schools, colleges, advocates, wholesalers, retailers operate around your branch? What are the commercial activities happening in their area of operation? That is the potential of the business opportunity available. I would also encourage them to check what the competitor is doing. Understanding what the competitor is doing—whether our products and services, customer approach, servicing, etc. in the market.

The other important thing is to assess how visible your branch is in the neighbourhood and how easily it is distinguished from other Banks. Many bankers fail to track this.

Train your leaders to lead. When Mr KR Kamath took over as Managing Director of Punjab National Bank, where I did a stint as Executive Director for over two years, he brought in a different energy. One day, he announced that he wanted to learn about banking from all the stalwarts in the banking industry and use their experience as a guiding hand.

We were lucky that we were exposed to several retired Chairmen and Managing Directors of Punjab National Bank. They all participated in our Top Management committee meetings and deliberated over our weekly performance. They also advised us on how to tackle business and personnel issues. This experiment paid off very well. It yielded great results in our HR practices; wherein we ensured that everybody promoted into Senior Management is exposed to Business Schools to start with. Our own senior leadership accompanied our promotees and set their expectations and training goals. We engaged XLRI, IIM Bangalore, Ahmedabad, Indore to conduct programmes for our Senior Executives. Even in our Business Plan meetings, we would invite external speakers who were prominent personalities in the Industry. We once had author Devdutt Patnaik, who shared his theories on leadership. We also invited Ms Ranjana Kumar, who shared with us her experience of turning around Indian Bank (Public Sector Bank) and as Vigilance Commissioner in Central Vigilance Commission.

The other thing we did was to encourage our own junior executives to speak about their own plans, how they would engage with customers, plan their bottom-up approach and so on. This interaction made our Business Plan meetings very effective. I tried this experiment very successfully in the Central Bank of India as well. Over a period, we realised that Branch Managers were more involved and committed to their own projections. So we used these Business Plan meeting to give inputs to the Regional and Zonal Managers so that they could prepare themselves properly. The vertical in charge would lead the discussion, followed by a few of the performing Regional Managers who would then give their inputs. This would be followed by some practical exercises and team contests based on the learnings of the day. This kind of engagement worked by invoking interaction and participation in problem solving. It helped us understand the effectiveness of the training and developed a lot of confidence in the teams. These exercises helped managers get a futuristic perspective on the opportunities around them.

I was also guided by my CMD then to always discuss problems and solutions with the Senior Managers before making my own recommendations. This helped me to view both the problem and solution from all perspectives, even the execution. This also meant Senior Managers became part of the solution process as well.

This engagement helped form a solid foundation for the implementation of the programmes we were planning. You may have a wonderful plan, but if your implementation plan does not have clarity, the project will fail. Now an implementation plan cannot be thrusted on the field office. It can be only prescribed by the Corporate Office, but when you align your thought process from the Corporate Office with the thought process of the field functionaries, it becomes a perfect execution plan. That is why the Regional Managers were made to deliver their own thought process and implementation ideas.

This way, there is more ownership from the team and you get the best results. A leader has to make sure that he or she is facilitating their people to deliver as per expectations; I term this initiative as empowerment, enablement, and then only demand performance.

Learn to manage your risk well. Risk is an intrinsic part of the DNA of a banker. In fact, banking is all about risk. Our economy can grow only with credit expansion. Credit expansion will happen only when lenders lend. But this lending has to happen to the right parties in the right manner. Only then will it yield returns for the bank as well as the economy. Therefore, bankers need to be enabled to take calculated risks. Risk Management is an important funtion of the banking industry.

I remember that I was once at a Work Conference in London. I met a journalist from the Asian Economist from Singapore. He had come to interview me. I remember having a long discussion with him on a positive outlook on the Indian economy, the future of the Punjab National Bank. It was a wonderful optimistic interview. However, when he was leaving, I remember that he said: "It is nice that you have this positive outlook. Please do not ignore that risk exists in everything. Even if the scenario is positive, you should not take things for granted."

It was a very useful piece of advice which I have always heeded.

The primary rule of Risk Management is that a banker must be able to identify risks, measure them, and learn how to mitigate those risks.

In the 90s, the Union Bank had a unique Credit Investigation Cell. The Branch Manager had to provide the name of the prospective borrowers of the customers—that is the buyers and sellers—and they would conduct a market intelligence study by visiting them and looking at their books. We would then get inputs on positives and negatives.

But each bank has its own processes. Now in my present assignment, as a strategic advisor of SWIFT India, for digitalization of Trade Finance, the Letter of Credit and Bank Guarantee are two areas where risk is underwritten at one particular point of time. But the risk occurs after a gap of maybe three months, six months, or one year, depending on the tenure of the instrument. There was no such policy which existed in the bank for monitoring these trade finance instruments. And thus, what happened in the banking industry, is that once you had done the credit assessment, uploaded the credit line and issued the bank guarantee or Letter of Credit, you only waited for the due date of that instrument and then started following up on whether the performance is getting serviced or whether the Letter of Credit is getting paid.

So the real problem crops up during the intermittent period where we do not engage with the monitoring part. If you are issuing a performance guarantee, then you should monitor performance on an ongoing basis so that there is no breach or default, and the guarantee doesn't get invoked. If you issue the letter of credit for 180 days, then you must see that when you open the import LC or domestic procurement LC for 180 days, the stocks are well-received, processed, converted into the final product, sold and receivables received.

While in Punjab National Bank we worked very hard getting all the learnings from the Non-Performing Assets, discussed with the field functionaries, and created the guidelines for monitoring of Letters of Credit and Bank Guarantees. Later on, I created a similar process for the Central Bank of India where the credit monitoring guidelines were not available for Trade Finance. These guidelines indicated how field staff should remain engaged with the life cycle of a borrower. When you are lending 75 percent, you have to be part of the transaction on an ongoing basis as a life cycle partner. So, that was a very big learning which we got on the risk management side.

In normal parlance, credit risk emanates right from the time you are contracting with the borrowing party. If you are not able to do proper due diligence at that point of time, you are incurring a big risk. In those days, we did not have any tools like Credit Bureaus or various structured and unstructured information.

The second risk is when you are disbursing the loan. One needs to ensure that you are disbursing for the right purpose, whether it is going to the right people, whether the genuine vendors are there and whether the pricing is right. A number of things need to be seen and examined, not only from the compliance perspective but also to ensure that direct payment is being made to a proper supplier.

That is the rule; Now if I do not do proper due diligence on who the supplier is, there is a possibility that this payment will go to a fraudulent supplier and the money will be diverted. That is why, at every stage, while handling the borrower account, whether small or big, stipulating the proper terms and conditions of the borrower's sanctions is important so that there are no lapses and loose ends in disbursement of credit.

Finally, when you are disbursing the credit, the right way of disbursement in banking parlance will ensure end use of funds. Whatever purpose you have identified in the sanction note, the fund should be used only for that purpose. Then only will it be justified that the committed kinds of assets get created and these assets will produce the desired kind of revenue and that the loan will be repaid.

Understand the borrower's life cycle. First, you identify the borrower, you sanction the credit, you lend to the borrower, the borrower uses those funds, he does the business, he generates the cash, makes a profit out of it. Out of that profit, he repays the borrowing. He services the interest out of it, and then he continues his business and grows his business. The profit he accrues should be not only adequate to repay the bank loan and interest, but also good enough to generate capital required for the future growth of the borrower.

As a banker, if I am not in a position to monitor the credit life cycle of a borrower, there is a possibility that I might incur a risk at any stage of the borrower.

Understand Domestic/International market risks. Understanding market risk is also very important. I say this from the perspective of treasury operations in the banking industry. In banking, we view deposits as raw material. This deposit is to be deployed either for lending, or it has to be invested in the Treasury. In the good old days, 40 percent of the assets used to be treasury assets; these days this ratio has reduced to about 20–25 percent, and the lending accordingly has increased from 50 to 60 percent to 75–80 percent. But the size of the Treasuries are as big as the banks. If you look at the treasury of a big sized bank, it may be bigger than the size of smaller banks. In the treasury operations, you are doing the operation either in equity, bonds, or different investments. These are all market-related instruments, where the price movements happen on day-in-day out basis. And thus the market risk has to be properly understood. In fact, the Reserve Bank of India prescribes internal control guidelines for treasury operations. And all treasuries have to follow those norms, including when to get out of the business, which is called the cut loss limit. You cannot sustain the loss for a long period in the treasury on the assumption that the market will bounce back. So at a point in time, you have to cut off and exit the transaction, even if it is at a loss.

Treasury operations are equally important because they contribute substantially to the profits of the bank. And thus, market risk is all-important. It also has a definite impact on the credit side because you have the deposits, which are at a particular price, and you are lending at a particular price.

Now, in the lending business, you also have some lending against Exports and Imports. And here, basically, your risk relates to the market rate of the Currency. And if it is a volatile currency, it will have an impact on your business by either paying more for imports or realizing less from exports proceeds.

The most important part, again from the treasury as well as operations perspective, is called the Asset Liability Management Risk. This is connected to the assets which Banks have with the Treasury. The deposits like Current/Savings and Term Deposits are to be put in different buckets depending on the behavioural pattern of the Current/Savings Account portfolio and the actual residual period of the Term Deposit. Similarly, the advances portfolio, that is working capital facilities/term loans are to be bifurcated based on the expected cash inflows and outflows. The entire purpose of the Asset Liability Management is to ensure that the bank as a whole does not have a liquidity crunch and can optimise the cost of deposits and maximise yield on advances and security. These finer aspects have also to be understood at the Branch/ Regional/Zonal Manager level so that they are consciously building the qualitative portfolio of assets and liabilities in their respective balance sheets.

Know your Investor. Apart from the customer and boss, another important stakeholder, as you rise on the banking ladder, is the Investor. This is a very different perspective that senior leaders in banking have to develop. While in the Union Bank of India, I had the opportunity to be part of the team that launched the bank's IPO in 2002. This was a sequel to the government's initiative of liberalisation and privatisation in 1991 and then the entry of private sector banks in 1994. Obviously, all the private sector banks were listed companies on the stock exchange and enjoyed diverse holdings from domestic as well as global investors. In fact, in most of the private sector banks, the global investments were much higher. But in public sector banks, global investment was restricted to 20 percent of the total equity, which is called the limit for Foreign Institutional Investors. I had the wonderful opportunity to represent our bank at the Investors' meeting in 2002. It was decided to list the Union Bank of India on the stock exchange and I was put in charge of the marketing for the state of Maharashtra.

I had to do a lot of marketing for the IPO by doing roadshows for Union Bank of India in different areas of Maharashtra. After the success of these roadshows, I got an opportunity to represent Union Bank of India at the Investors' Conference in London, which was hosted by ABN Amro Bank. And I had a one-on-one meeting with various Investors in London as well as Edinburgh.

After Union Bank went public in 2002, we had to showcase what the bank was doing to create value for investors. Every listed bank had to conduct an Analysts'/Investors' meeting after the results were declared. In that analyst meeting, typically the investor world likes to come and understand what the bank is doing. This was normally done in India for domestic investors, while global investors could join virtually. Here, the bank's CMD, and the entire management team, present themselves and talk about the various initiatives they have undertaken, the various productivity numbers, efficiency numbers, so on and so forth.

As a General Manager of the bank, I had the opportunity to attend these meetings which were held for analysts after the quarterly and annual results. I also attended a couple of International Meetings in

New York and Singapore. This experience of coordinating for these meetings helped me when I took over as Executive Director of Punjab National Bank in 2009.

To be very frank, as General Manager, you might be only decorating the dais, but as Executive Director and CMD, you are actually making presentations as well as responding to various queries posed by the analysts and the investors. Having said that, in Punjab National Bank, I got an opportunity to attend the analyst meeting, as I said, every quarter.

What does a leader in banking learn from these meets? Many lessons. Typically, when you make a presentation at such meetings, what exactly is the investor world expecting of you? The investor world expects us to understand how you are doing value creation for shareholders. When you talk of value creation, it means that if I have invested maybe at a face value of Rs 10 or if I bought the share from the market at Rs 50 or Rs 100, what is the upside I am giving to the investor after he buys the shares?

Obviously, the upside gets measured by a very basic parameter: the book value of the share and the price on the stock exchange. If your price to book value is more than one, which means positive, every investor feels that his or her investment is secured. This sounds easy but, in reality, is not easy to deliver. Unfortunately, one sees many bank shares that run below price to book value, which is less than one.

This means that there is value deterioration. This means loss for the investor. I was in Punjab National Bank between 2009 and 2011, and it was one of the best periods in the banking industry in terms of various productivity and efficiency parameters.

When we talk of the productivity parameters, typically we talk in terms of what is the productivity per employee, or the business mix per employee or to understand each individual component of the business, which is deposits and advances, per employee.

When you talk of deposits and advances, it is absolutely essential to determine the quality of the composition of deposits and advances. This has a direct bearing on the profitability of the bank. If the quality of your deposit is very good, it means your CASA (Current and Savings Account deposits) proportion is higher. Typically, in Public Sector banks, our CASA proportion used to be more than 40 percent, which in those days, even for the HDFC Bank and the ICICI Bank, may be 45 to 50 percent. The advantage of CASA being high is that your cost of deposit is low.

If your cost of deposit is low, you get a better spread, because typically the yield on advances is market-driven, although your BPLR (Benchmark Prime Lending Rate) could differ from other banks. Now it is moved to MCLR (Marginal Cost of the Fund- based Lending Rate).

Investors consider this when they look at the size but also the quality of deposits. This means your proportion of current accounts and savings accounts should be a reasonable proportion of more than 40 percent and your total fixed deposits should also not be very skewed into higher buckets.

I'll give you a typical example: one can achieve a bigger size of deposits by going in for a bulk deposit. There was a time in the banking industry when we used to bid for bulk deposits. It means we used to bid at a higher rate than what the competitors could quote. Now, if you have a composition of such a deposit, it is a drag on your cost of deposit. So, while it will push your deposit higher, the cost is also higher. Any such composition of a deposit was never seen positively by the Investors.

The Investor is only interested in what kind of value creation you are delivering to your shareholders. The shareholders get value only when there is a qualitative approach by the banks to ensure that their quantity is not growing at the cost of quality and there is a right-directional approach to the quality as well as the quantity of business.

Having said that, when it comes to advances, the composition should be well-diversified in terms of risk. They want to check the quality of your advance or asset portfolio. So the most important part in the composition of the advances is how the risk is diversified in terms of per party exposure, in terms of sectoral exposure, so on and so forth.

What Investors would look at is whether the bank has created a well-diversified portfolio so that if there is a risk occurrence in one particular sector of the industry, it is not impacted very badly. Because if you've got a concentration risk, diversification is the only way to minimise it.

A senior banker needs to have a proper understanding of the growth sectors where risk is measured not only in the short term but also in the medium term. He or she also needs to understand how these sectors are likely to behave in the next two to three years' time. Typically, when you sit across the Investors, they would like to understand how far bankers understand this business of banking, as well as any other sector, like Power or Renewable Energy or Coal or Mining, etc.

Investors are very careful when banks are putting money into Public Sector entities, which are not considered to be very efficient investments. Of course, efficient PSUs do exist.

I'll give you one very important example. Many banks have invested very heavily in DISCOMs, which are the energy/electricity distribution companies for the Electricity Boards in every State. Those investments have come very heavily on all banks. Those investments have turned non-performing for various reasons connected to State Government interventions like non-payment of subsidies, leakage in power transmission etc.

And thus the investor world would like to have a complete dissection—sectoral, geographical, owner-wise dissection—of a bank's portfolios. From this data, they assess whether the bank is doing good risk management and will be able to sustain the profitability they have earned now.

My experience of interacting with global investors in New York, London and Singapore, helped me understand how they assess our businesses. There are many Indians abroad who are important consultants to the investing world in domestic quarters as well as globally. It has helped me to connect and talk with these consultants who understand our country slightly better than foreign consultants would. I mean, an Indian consultant living abroad would have a completely different perspective on Indian banking than an American who has never visited India. Many of these Indian consultants who represent global investment companies understand very well how the system is, how things really happen, particularly in a public sector bank or private sector bank.

Investors also study market share and the bank's plans to improve it. They will check how competitive your marketing strategy is. They review your productivity per employee and per business unit. So if my bank is operating 5000 branches, they will want to study how many of the branches are doing above average business and whether their profitability is in line with the bank's overall profitability. They also want to understand how the team will drive each strategic business unit or cost centre to become a profit centre. Typically, around 70–80 percent of branches should be profitable.

When they consider numbers, they compare peer banks of the same size. So a Union Bank of India will be compared to other public sector banks of the same size.

Usually speaking, these Investor meets are scheduled by agencies in India who aggregate all global Investors and invite bankers to present their cases, as potential players where investment could be attracted. Surprisingly, the Investors had already done a background check and reviewed the balance sheets and done their homework on the complete banking environment. They are not interested in number crunching but in how the banks are preparing for their way forward or addressing business problems.

KYB: Know your borrower. Now, if your stake is 75 percent in the borrower's unit, you have got to understand the business well and where things go wrong, when the business is not conducted in the spirit of the situation. We also need to understand if borrower is not able to conduct business as expected because of various external factors and how to correct that situation.

You should be compliant, you should be cautious. And you should be extremely engaged with the activity you are doing. Because you can't become a Branch Manager without knowing the business, without knowing the customer. KYC is not only paperwork. You have to know your customer beyond the papers. So I have coined a word KYB. Know your borrower.

Even when I was Branch Manager at Rewa branch and Bhopal, I had the practice of visiting our borrowers at their workplace. I would visit them, check their factories or offices. I would try and understand their operations, challenges. For my agricultural borrowers, I tried to understand how farming is done, how wells are dug, who their neighbours are. I could gel with the shopkeepers; I would spend time at their shops.

I would say even KYB is also not enough. You have to know your borrower's customer also that is KYBC.

KYC to KYB to KYBC. It means what happens if I am a borrower, but I have sold the goods to 10 customers and 5 out of them have defaulted? I have not done proper due diligence on those customers. And because of their default, I have become a defaulter with the bank. The borrower may put his hands up and say I don't care. But the banker cannot. He has a responsibility to the stakeholders. You have got to know who is your borrower's customer and supplier. It is what you call a supply chain assessment in today's terminology.

When I was in the Overseas branch in Opera House, Mumbai, we once had a customer, who was not from the specific community typically known for driving diamond business, who applied for a loan for diamond business. But I knew the diamond business traders locally and I knew this customer. I knew that he had no experience and no set up to do the diamond processing at his place. I was aware that he was only into trading activities. So I rejected that application. I have rejected many such loans when I have observed inconsistencies in the papers or in the people.

Or maybe you can say that bankers also sometimes are unable to really truly perceive or sense the risk in the operations. Despite everything being in place, diversion of funds may happen or a borrower may misrepresent some information. And thus, it is very essential that when you are a banker, you should not be scared of all these situations. You should be very diligent/transparent.

It is therefore important to create a proper culture of understanding the risk at all levels. People need to be sensitised that risk is inherent but that it needs to be mitigated in the right manner. Taking risk is a basic dharma for a banker.

In the early days, bankers did not have the wherewithal to assess risk correctly. If we needed to know if a particular person is a borrower of any other bank, I would send that borrower with a No Dues certificate on paper. The borrower would go to all banks and get it stamped and signed. There was no way to tell if it was forged or not.

Today, this situation is different. We have Credit Bureaus and Data Science Companies and analytics available in the system. This simplifies a lot of the processes for lenders. Today, bankers and lenders just need to do their due diligence on the system. If you believe you are the CEO of your branch or department, the simple process of due diligence and proper governance is extremely crucial to all your work and also your career as a banker. Let me explain in the next chapter.

Chapter 8

Follow your CEO Instinct

It is an ongoing debate whether Risk Management is a tick box compliance formality or has to be a culture of the Organisation. I have participated in a number of such discussions where ultimately, if you just do it as a tick box compliance, you are not really mitigating the risk correctly. To a large extent, credit risk is about individual perception of the manager processing it. But guidelines are extremely important as well. The guidelines are more like safeguards which have been created for our own protection. Complying just for the sake of it because you want to go ahead, ultimately defeats the purpose of risk mitigation.

I had the opportunity to visit London in 2009 for an event for Institute of Directors, that hosted a competition for the bankers. Such events were really crucial to build visibility for our banks internationally. That year, the contest was about HR initiatives. And I remember that the PNB had participated in that competition. I was asked to make a presentation to the jury of Institute of Directors, and we were selected as the best bank in that year. And we were invited to London to receive that award. At the time, I also visited our subsidiary and hosted a Board Meeting. In banking, when you are visiting any foreign subsidiary or foreign country, one of the most important activities which we are expected to do is connect with the investors' world. We hosted the investors meeting which was attended by all the global Investors. At the event, there was a lot of discussion and curiosity around how global meltdown would impact India and how Indian banking would handle it. It was a great lesson for us. The reason was that, that year the NPA ratios had come down to as low as 2%. Between 2002 and 2006, the banking industry had addressed its very high NPA ratios extremely well, using various tools like SARFAESI (Securitisation and Reconstruction of Financial Assets and Enforcement of Securities Act) and DRT (Debt Recovery Tribunal) Act to expedite recoveries. That had brought the NPA ratios to a very respectable level. It was a big learning for me that our efforts at managing NPAs were very reassuring to the global Investors that our banks took these compliances seriously. Infact Investors were keen to know whether Government will increase the limit for Foreign Institutional Investors over existing limit of 20% for Public Sector Banks.

To reiterate, we are not merely lenders, we are a partner in the business to the amount and extent that we are lending. If you have lent 75% you are a partner to that extent. So you need to be involved in that account as well.

Put it all on paper. One such situation was when I was the Chief Manager in the Overseas branch, Mumbai, between 1996 to 1999. And I had a customer who was into pharmaceuticals and was essentially a trader, exporting to Russia and other countries. He had a well established business and very good connections. And thus, he could procure the goods very well and export them. In the late 90s, exports were considered to be a very important activity because the foreign exchange reserves in the country were almost nil in 1991. And various promotional activities were done by the government and the bankers to promote exports. So this customer was having a packing credit facility. In order to give packing credit facility, you have to have a sanctioned limit. Secondly, you need an underlying contract with the party to whom you are paying the amount of the packing credit limit. I had released a substantial amount of around Rs 1 crore from the party's packing credit account to one of the manufacturer supplier in Mumbai. The payment was made to the manufacturer party directly, but my customer clandestinely took some 50% of the money from them for other purposes. Hence, the party did not supply the required goods in time. The export did not happen as committed, and the packing credit account became a bad account. Obviously, the moment the account is termed bad, the investigation begins. Through proper interrogation of the other party, I discovered that the money was paid to our customer.

I was also given a show cause notice and asked by the management to give an explanation. Thankfully, I was highly transparent in all my transactions and all my efforts to safeguard the bank's money. I was able to give a satisfactory explanation of all the efforts I took, along with the documentation. My show cause was closed after proper investigation. The investigation proved that this was a fraud committed by the party, and a legal case was filed. Luckily, we had security; he had a flat in Napean Sea Road which was held with us as security, and we sold that and recovered the money.

But this is where my KYBC comes into picture. Although I knew that the customer of my borrower is a very strong manufacturer, but the relationship between the two was fraudulent. So even our instinct needs to be sharper.

How will you find out if everything with a customer is above board? This means we need to inspect the goods at the site of the manufacturer and be able to inspect the manufacturing cycle as well and whether the goods are supplied in the stipulated period. As a banker, you have a responsibility to ensure that your money is getting properly utilised at the end of the manufacturer-supplier as well, so that there is some kind of mechanism to verify.

When a banker is transparent in all dealings and complies with all the paperwork, he or she can duly attend to these kinds of situations.

There was another such case that was against my senior. This was in the late 90s. He was the General Manager in charge of the Mumbai zone. We have a typical activity called ship-breaking that is done in the Darukhana area of Mumbai. It's an activity where the ship breakers buy ships which are meant to be scrapped. These ships are parked in the ports for some time, are broken up into scrap and then sold part by part. Monitoring of this kind of activity was based on trust in those days, but it was not blind trust. We had many checks and balances in place. But still my Chairman thought that it was the fault of the General Manager, and there was a lack of monitoring that led to giving room for the borrower to play. There was an enquiry against this General Manager, and the case was handled by the Central Vigilance Commissioner. I was in charge of the Recovery Department then. Since I am from the field, I understood this case very well and I was the management representative in this enquiry.

Now there is a big responsibility on the management representative. You have to withstand and prove what your management has claimed in the enquiry. At the same time, you have to show total transparency on the operations side. And let me tell you, I was grilled sufficiently by the independent inquiry officer from the vigilance commission. I assured them that whatever had gone wrong was beyond the reach of the General Manager. And believe me, with my proper articulation, and because I knew the business issues and operations so deeply, I was able to support our side well. Our General Manager was discharged of all the charges.

There is always a Sword of Damocles hanging over the necks of public sector bankers: the three Cs; Central Bureau of Investigation (CBI), Central Vigilance Commissioner (CVC) and Comptroller Audit General (CAG). All bankers are exposed to this risk.

The Nirav Modi scam is a prime example of how people can misuse the authority given to them in pushing fraudulent messages, establishing Letter of Credit and allowing the party to withdraw the funds against a fraudulent Letter of Credit. The challenge is the operational risk.

A lot of checks and balances were introduced to ensure that all the transactions had the approval of at least two people, the maker and the checker, to manage such risks.

Why do NPAs happen

Now if banks are indeed sticking to the guidelines, then why do the Advances turn into NPAs in the first place? Primarily, we need to understand that any non-performing asset could be because of various reasons; external, internal or behavioural reasons. Despite banks having all the checks and balances in place, if there is a deliberate diversion of funds happening by camouflaging some transactions, it can't be controlled.

But what is possible is that a banker is engaged right from identifying and onboarding a customer with all the due diligence done, not only in letter but also in spirit. If you are drawing a credit score from the credit bureaus, do you just refer to what is the score, and go ahead? Or do you go through the report and apply your mind to figure out what could be the behavioural challenges of this client if he is not performing? You have to always envisage and map the risk.

The risk management has got 3 Ms, that is, Mapping, Measuring and Mitigation. But these tools have to be applied not only for compliance sake but also in spirit. There is a list of checks and balances, but the banker will have to study beyond this tick box compliance. This is where the behavioural science comes into picture. As a lender, you must refer to multiple databases to really understand a borrower beyond his credit score. This is how data science companies prove useful. I have been associated with the Rubix data science company, and I am always amazed at what the data can reveal about consumers and their behaviour.

Here we collect the databases for all MSMEs or corporate world much, much beyond Credit Bureaus. Today you have got the information about whether the borrrower has paid the Employee's Provident Fund, GST and Income Tax regularly, and if there are any court cases against him. So, the point is that every lender should look at how they can do proper due diligence to establish that these risks are not there.

See, the very simple thing if somebody has failed in depositing the Provident Fund of employees, it means he is having a liquidity constraint. Now, with a company having a liquidity constraint, there is a possibility that they may play with the system when you are assessing for credit lines. So every banker today is expected to get into the root cause analysis of any problem which you come across. As I said initially, NPAs do not occur just because somebody wants it to happen deliberately. There could be various internal reasons of mismanagement.

It could be external events also, like market related activities. See, I am in the business, but today the demand for that particular product has reduced. What do I do? I am in a business where the product is getting imported from countries like China, which are dumping the market, which causes prices to crash. In that case, even if your production cost is higher, you will be forced to sell the goods at a much lower price and incur losses. This factor will not be in the borrower's control.

Now, in such situations, things do go wrong, thus it needs efficient NPA management in all the sectors of lending such as agriculture sector, MSME sector, corporate sector and infrastructure sector. It is very essential that the causes of the non-performing asset be analysed and understood properly, and corrective actions are taken accordingly. The corrective actions should be taken in good time, and that is why the Reserve Bank of India has introduced the concept of the SMA, that is the Special Mentioned Account, where the default is identified within 30 days and corrective action is expected to be taken in 30 to 60 days.

So, while the NPA is recognised on account of the 90 days of default, you have got 90 days to ensure that either you recover the default amount, or you identify the causes of the default and bring out a solution. As a banker, I very strongly feel that my primary responsibility is to understand the causes and find out the solution and take corrective measures. If there is a deliberate default, you have to immediately act without waiting for 90 days, call back the account, notify the borrower that he has done wrong, and take recovery measures immediately.

Non-Compliance can impact your career. Here, I would like to narrate a couple of incidents that prove why compliance is important. While I was in charge of the Mumbai zone, a fantastic proposal came to my hand. There was a person who got a license from the Government of Maharashtra to operate radio cabs. In 2006, radio cabs were not very popular; there were only Meru cabs at the time. This was a competitor. So, we studied this proposal extremely well. The Government of Maharashtra had approved it and had invited me as a lender to discuss this proposal. And it was notified by the government for licensing to a unit and then after all the scrutiny, we approved it as a commercial proposal. Not only did we approve it, but we also leveraged it for publicity. All the 100 cabs to be launched were to be flagged off by the then Chief Minister of Maharashtra. This project meant that cab drivers would get the extra income, and the bank would help in their self-reliance.

Everything went well. But there was a promoter who did not have genuine capital with him and tried to play with the system. He imported the cab meters from Singapore, but the invoice that he submitted to us was an inflated one. And against the 100 pieces of meters, he took delivery of 50 pieces only. The Meru representatives found this and complained against this man, me, our Branch Manager and Regional Manager. This case affected us for almost 3 years. I was interrogated at the Vigilance Commissioner level. Thankfully, my management had total confidence in my ethics, credibility and objective credit decisions.

This was purely an operational issue, where the Branch Manager should have been a little more vigilant to spot this because the sanctioning authority can't be the operational authority. Thankfully, our documentation and proofs helped state our case.

A more serious incident happened with me when I was Deputy General Manager, in charge of the Bombay Samachar Marg branch. In my stint at this branch, I was very committed and conscious in the recovery and reduction of NPAs. There was still a problematic non-performing asset. The NPA borrower had a flat in a building on Marine Drive that was mortgaged with our bank. After repeated reminders and actions, it was almost time to sell the flat for recovery of funds. The process was on, and the decision was coming in the bank's favour. This customer came to me and offered a cheque for $1,00,000/- (1 lakh dollars). He requested that I just put the cheque in clearing and stop the proceedings for the flat sale. I found this very fishy. I immediately said that I did not trust the cheque and I would not accept it. After months of follow up, how could an exporter-importer like him produce such funds so quickly? I refused the cheque. How could I be sure that the cheque was genuine? I refused to stop my action of recovery also. I told him that if he was so confident, he could go to another bank, clear the cheque and transfer the money to me.

This customer went to a Cooperative Bank, opened an account there and deposited this cheque for $1,00,000/-. The bank presented it in clearing without knowing any of the implications. This cheque came into the clearing house, which was managed by the State Bank of India, and it got reported to the Reserve Bank of India. The RBI started an investigation into this. As part of this investigation, the Reserve Bank got to know that initially this cheque was shown to me as DGM of the Union Bank of India. And under FEMA guidelines, I was under the obligation to inform the Reserve Bank immediately if I was privy to any doubtful transaction.

Although it was not a deliberate mistake or ignorance, as a banker, I had a liability under FEMA to report that cheque. The then Reserve

Bank Deputy Governor called my CMD, and ordered immediate suspension from duties. My CMD, Mr. Leeladhar, who thereafter became the Deputy Governor of RBI, called me and tried to understand all the process part of it from me. He totally understood my point of view and did try to explain to the Deputy Governor that there was no need for suspension. He knew that I had a good track record and that my integrity was always above board. He explained that my suspension would send a very wrong message in the Organisation. Unfortunately, he had no choice but to remove me from the post. After clarification, he transferred me to the Corporate Office. He also called my wife and explained to her the situation properly, so that my family was not demoralised. I was asked to hand over the charge of my office and to report the next day as DGM Recovery.

Recovery: The Lifeline

This was in 2002, SARFAESI (Securitization and Reconstruction of Financial Assests and Enforcement of Security Interest Act) was implemented for the first time by the Reserve Bank of India. That was the year when the gross Non Performing Assets (NPA) in the banking industry were very high and the RBI came out with the non-discriminatory, non-discretionary, one-time settlement (OTS) scheme. There was no laxity in that; neither the borrower nor the bank had any room to say anything. We worked very hard to bring down the NPAs. And after a year, on account of my good performance, I was transferred as Regional Manager for Mumbai RO South, which happens to be the largest Region of the Bank.

The point of sharing this incident is that it is not enough to work with our instincts. Be conscious of what decisions you are making and why. Had I been little conscious about FEMA and my obligation beyond banking, to the society and to my stakeholders, this incident could have been totally avoided. In today's world, a banker has to be aware of his or her responsibility for the environment, society and governance. This duty is as important as his or her banking duties. That is the first lesson that I learnt there.

Earn credibility and integrity, and the rewards will follow. The second lesson is that if your boss has trusted you and given you the responsibility with all the trust, then your responsibility to deliver and maintain your credibility is very high. It is the trust and the credibility that I built in my past profiles that worked in my favour in the crisis I faced.

The people in my organisation trusted me and that brings in the rewards in the long term. My subsequent posting as a Regional Manager in the biggest region of the country is testament that every performer gets rewarded. There is a wrong notion unfortunately that people get rewarded for *chamchagiri* or for their relationships. Good performance never goes unrewarded. In my case, the very fact that the CMD of a bank upheld his decision not to suspend me and convinced the Deputy Governor of RBI on his perspective itself is a proof. This is also because Mr Leeladhar had his own credibility in the Reserve Bank of India. They believed him as well. And that is how the messaging goes in the organisation.

They say that every banker needs to be scared of the three Cs: Central Vigilance Commission, Central Bureau of Investigation and Comptroller and Auditor General. I personally do not think one needs to be scared of anything if one is ensuring all the compliances and doing their due diligence properly. It is also important to articulate what our understanding of the situation and operations is.

The biggest challenge in a banker's career is that he has to take the credit decision. I call this a challenge because the behaviour of that decision does not totally depend on his credit decision, but on various factors right from the intent of the borrower, to the internal issues of the project, or the external issues of the environment in which the project has to survive and become viable and generate necessary cash flows. Unfortunately, in hindsight, any credit decision can be proved to be wrong. And thus in a banker's career, it is extremely important that he always takes care of transparency in all his or her dealings.

The best lending decisions are bottom-up and not top-down. When I say that a lender is a partner of the client, it is not the General Manager who is a partner, it is the Branch Manager on the field who is the partner. This Branch Manager is the one who has to understand day-in-day-out operational difficulties. And it is at the behest of the Branch Manager that the Corporate Offices of the Banks who approve the loan.

Whatever decision a manager is taking, he or she should be able to put it on a paper besides the normal compliance which is required to be done as per the circulars of the bank. There is no single decision, which is on a very firm footing and that fully falls within a given framework. There will always be some or other kind of deviations. And therefore, the Branch, Regional, or General Manager, who is taking that particular credit decision, should himself or herself be satisfied with that decision.

Even if somebody from the top management would ask, I would always satisfy myself as a manager on whether that credit decision is correct. The proposal has to be understood by the people who have to handle the borrower and the proposal, and then handle the industry post disbursement of loan.

I will give another personal example here. At the Union Bank, our proposals would go to the Central Office; this proposal would have the details of the particular facility, a particular amount and so on. And the Central Office would sanction a different amount. At that time, this was just communicated through a sanction letter from the Central Office. I would often argue with my General Manager (Credit) that I had prepared a proposal giving all my logic and rationale. Although it was their prerogative to sanction what they want, it was my right to understand why the amount I pitched for was not sanctioned. It would be important to understand where have I gone wrong in understanding and how the central office process decided on such proposals.

My plea went up to the Chairman level and soon the Bank introduced the system that, along with the sanction note, a process note would also be submitted to the field functionaries so that they should understand how their proposal was assessed and processed at the Central Office level and what were the reasons that impacted their decisions.

Typically, the perception is that if the boss says, then the branch does it. If the Chairman says, then the General Manager does it. If you are a true banker, you have got to understand the business and its operations before you decide to get into the business. And before you do what the higher-ups have said, you have to do all the due diligence and be satisfied yourself that it is a sound business decision.

If you are able to justify your decision and record it, it is extremely helpful. And even though I had a couple of hassles in my career, I could withstand all the hassles only because I had made it a habit that whatever decision I took, I should be recording that why I felt this decision was right or should be taken.

In the credit department, my mentor was Mr. R Venkatramani, who retired as a General Manager from the Union Bank of India. He was very thorough in credit practices. He used to tell me, "Mohan, even if you are murdering somebody, you should be able to defend it till the last. If you are able to prove that you murdered in the cause of your own safety, even the law will not punish you. Similarly, when you're making a credit decision, you should not leave anything to the interpretation of people."

He taught me that even beyond the normal compliance framework, one should be able to put our remarks as to why those decisions have been taken. And that is why I have always maintained copious notes on everything I do.

I was privileged to have mentoring from all my CMDs Mr V Leeladhar, Mr Cherian Varghese, Mr M V Nair and Mr K R Kamath, the Executive Directors Mr Venugopal, Mr T Y Prabhu, Mr R S Reddy and Mr S Raman and my General Managers like Mr K V Shyamsunder, former Field General Manager, Mumbai, Mr M S Sundarrajan, who retired as the CMD of the Indian Bank, and Mr. B D Narang, who retired as CMD of the Oriental Bank of Commerce, and Mr V Sridhar, former CMD, United Commercial Bank, Mr K L Gopal Krishanan, former ED of Corporation Bank, who have also guided me that decision-making is easier if you maintain the transparency. They taught me that a banker cannot dissociate himself or herself from their credit decisions if he or she wants to grow.

Personally, I believe these decisions are easier if one has a strong sense of ethics. I will explain what I mean.

Go with your values. There are those in banking who have preferred to play it safe: they do not go to the field, so that they do not have to take any credit decisions, and their files are always clean. If you are not taking credit decisions, there is no likelihood of you getting a charge sheet. But that is not right or ethical either. Bankers should be credit-cautious and not credit-averse. We are in that position to lend a helping hand so that business and society can prosper. Lending is our *dharma*. The ethical thing to do is informed lending. I have to be sensitive to the various risks associated.

When you are led by your values and integrity, there is not a lot that can go wrong. Values and ethics serve two objectives. First, they are a guiding light in all your transactions. It is my parents who have inculcated these values in my everyday behaviour. I am not a person who could reconcile to any wrongdoings. And when you are led by those values, there is never any doubt or indecision.

Let me narrate to you a simple incident from my early years. The first challenge to my values and ethics came when I was Branch Manager at Rewa. The branch had big customers who would try enticements during Diwali, Dussehra and other festivals. Once a very old gentleman came home to meet me and my wife. While leaving, he gave a sweet packet to my wife, saying, Here are some sweets for the kids. We were living in housing board quarters. When I went out to accompany him to his car, my wife opened the packet to see what sweets were there. She saw there was money in it. She was very angry. When I returned, she immediately showed me the packet and asked me to return it. I ran out and caught the customer just as he had started driving away. I returned the sweets box and said, "You have misunderstood me. I respect your age, but this is a crime. I cannot accept this bribe. Please take this away and never do this again."

Imagine what a blessing it is that even my wife shared my values. If she had not immediately objected or coerced me to take that money, I would have inadvertently been seen as accepting a bribe without realising it. Sticking to these values is what has helped me grow and not regret any of my decisions. You may lose out monetarily, but you will always have the satisfaction of having lived a good life.

Secondly, values and ethics impact both your relationships and credibility in the organisation. This is not only about bribes but even about standing for what you believe in. My mentors and bosses had confidence in me because of my conduct and not because I was a *chamcha* or a yes-man. Values help you create visibility for yourself. Your leaders need performers and not *chamchas. Chamchas* are for short term benefit, while performers are for the long term. I take the pride to myself on being a performer. It took a long time to build this credibility; I spent over 20 years as a Branch Manager, and then Regional Manager and then Zonal Manager which earned me tremendous credibility. And I could do this because I viewed banking as my *DHARMA*.

Today, the business of lending has changed drastically. I am happy to say that even after my retirement, I continue fulfilling my lending dharma through my work on many digital banking and lending ventures.

Digitisation has led to a true revolution in banking which I will take you through in the next chapter.

Chapter 9

The Onset of Digitisation

Digitisation has really gone a long way in revolutionising the banking system. The first advantage of digitisation has been the access to customer data. After completion of Core Banking, banks had a bird's eye view of customer behaviour centrally. At one glance, we could understand how many home loans were disbursed, what percentage of these were standard home loans and how many were bad loans. Various stages of digitisation helped us understand demography-wise, geography-wise, district-wise numbers and pointed us to where the actual business potential was so that we could focus our efforts on those areas. This could be for purposes of Deposit Mobilisation, which is term deposits, savings or current deposits as well as potential for expanding credit.

Monitor The NPAs

The other area where digitisation helped was monitoring NPAs. When there was no system-driven process to identify NPAs, there was a lot of room for bankers to hide it or manage it. Therefore the correct picture was not emerging at times. Now the biggest advantage of digitisation was that NPAs get identified 100% through system-driven logic. When you get the correct picture of the non-performing asset, the banks drive their own processes to address NPAs. Today, accounts get identified at the zero SMA level. SMA stands for Special Mentioned Account where the account gets flagged immediately after the date of non-payment. So the account gets monitored first day onward. So there is SMA 0, there is SMA 1 that is one month onwards. SMA 2, that is second month onwards.

After three months, it is called a non-performing asset, where you get 90 days room to really monitor and follow up with the borrower for the recovery. Here technology has helped reach and follow up with the customer as well as understand what are the reasons because of which customer is not able to pay. This helps every banker analyse whether this default is on account of his own behaviour or deliberate attempt not to pay or there are external reasons. I mean, COVID was the biggest learning here where many customers created a big picture of not being able to pay their loan instalments. When the customer poses this problem bankers must have a tool to verify that information.

And to that end, Credit Bureaus have come very handy. Every Credit Bureau in the country brings out analysis which is industry-wise or pincode wise. For instance, what is the behaviour of customers in a particular pincode. Now if a particular customer from a particular pincode says he has a problem but the behaviour of the others in that geography or demography is good, the banker can question or monitor him. But I will reiterate that technology alone cannot solve this problem. The banker has to personally monitor as well. If after one month also, the customer is not coming forward, the Bank Branch staff has to visit the customer's place. If it is personal loan or home loan or whatever, you have to visit the place and the person.

Technology cannot replace a personal touch but it has gone a long way in spotting NPAs, as well as in promoting Deposit Mobilization, and using Depositor's information for selling other retail products and services.

Taking A Look At Trade Finance Digitisation

Beyond this the banks have also gone into digitisation of Trade Finance products like Letter of Credit and Bank Guarantee. Organisations like

SWIFT India, which I am representing as a Strategic Consultant, or NESL, which is under the IBC as Information Utility Center, have simplified these to a large extent. It is extremely cumbersome when the customer has to maintain the physical papers, stamp duty paid with non-judicial stamp and so on. Recently I was amazed to read about a Telgi-like scam in New Delhi. Telgi scam happened in Nasik in mid-90s, forging non-judicial stamps in different denominations for crores of rupees. Now despite technology, if this scam can be repeated in today's age, digitisation is the only answer. Printing of non-judicial stamp should stop at the state level and bankers should be mandated not to use the non-judicial stamp for the issuance of bank guarantee. There is always a push-pull angle to such regulations. The push comes from the regulator, from the government side, from the bank side and the pull comes from the benefits, which accrues to the customers.

Now let's talk about customers like NSE, BSE or Customs who get thousands of bank guarantees every month. These bank guarantees come to the organisation in physical format, imagine how much storage you need. Not only that, when you get it in physical format, you have to convert it into digital and store it in that format. You have to collect the important information to create the MIS. Your ERP does not absorb it automatically.

But there are now products which are being given by SWIFT India or other Fintech organisations where complete end-to-end digitisation is possible. These bank guarantees can be stamped digitally, pushed digitally and entire information is created as metadata which goes into ERP directly for the purpose of MIS and monitoring.

However, the most important gift of digitisation has been predominantly on the payment side. Payment systems in the banking industry started evolving somewhere from 2008 when the National Payment Corporation of India (NPCI) was conceived.

It got incorporated in 2009. I had the opportunity of being a Committee member for the payment and settlement Committee of Reserve Bank with Mr. Padmanabhan in 2007. Because of that, I was also on the board of NPCI's first board incorporated in 2009.

Now, National Payment Corporation of India started providing payment products like RTGS, NEFT, IMPS, and the last being the UPI, around 2016 which has served the purpose of smaller denominations payments helping in replacement of cash. These products have simplified banking so much that UPI has become a globally accepted product where global giants like Singapore and few other European countries have tied up with this payment system to enable even cross-border remittances to happen seamlessly.

Modern payment systems have evolved from a unique position of customer-centricity. India is bestowed with a large population of non-resident Indians who would be looking for payment solutions to send money to their families seamlessly. Till a decade ago, this was a frustrating experience. Today payments can be made both ways without hassle.

These days I am so happy, when we go to the market, if you want to buy vegetables, you can pay by using a QR code. Using UPI, PayTM and G-Pay have drastically changed how small transactions take place in the country. Now the real question is: has this penetrated rural India? Is digitisation benefiting the small businessman in villages or the farmers? Financial inclusion is a long-cherished dream that digitisation is enabling in today's world.

Many Corporate Business Correspondents are delivering these services through network of retailers in rural India.

Every year India achieves more and more milestones in Financial Inclusion. As a goal, Financial Inclusion and Inclusive Growth is an agenda that was kickstarted way before computerisation or digitisation took place. This was in the form of the Lead Bank Scheme and the formation of the Regional Rural Banks.

Reaching The Last Mile

The objective of the nationalization of banks in India in 1969 itself was to ensure that the banks should reach to the last mile and have an inclusive approach for the growth. With that purpose in mind, the initial initiative was for opening of the branches country-wide. To start with, there was a Dantwala Committee which came out with the guidelines that every district in the country should be owned by one or the other bank. This was called the Lead Bank Scheme, under which all the districts in the country had been allotted a responsibility to one or the other nationalised bank. And the role of that lead bank, was to set up an office of Lead District Manager in the lead district.

Till date, every lead district has got a Lead District Manager. The role of this lead district manager is to associate with the District Collector, who is the chairperson for the District Level Consultative Committee, which gets represented by all the bankers who are present in the district, be it Public Sector banks, or Private Sector banks, Cooperative or Foreign banks; they are all supposed to be participating as a representative. The primary drive of the district level consultative committee was to create a district level credit plan which outlined how exactly the credit growth should happen and which are the areas where the credit deployment is required to take place going forward and accordingly checking the capacity of the Banks with respect to projects which are coming up in the district and other potential opportunities. The district level credit consultative committee will come out with the district credit plan; the targets are assigned to different banks based on that credit plan, which includes agriculture growth, financing of MSMEs, Industrial or Infrastructure sector and so on.

Riding On Rural Initiatives

The Union Bank of India was privileged to have four Regional Rural Banks in Uttar Pradesh; two in Kerala and one in Madhya Pradesh. I had the opportunity to work in the lead districts of Rewa and Sidhi when the Rewa Sidhi Grameen Bank was launched. So that was the second initiative to reach the villages in Bharat. In banking, our offerings are very different when it comes to Bharat and when it comes to India. When we live in metros, we can say we are in India. But think of those 7 lakh villages where our large number of people live in more than 30–40 crore households in this country. Much before the Pradhan Mantri Jan Dhan Yojana was announced, in 1974–1975, the Government of India embarked on two major lending schemes.

The first was the Differential Interest Rate Scheme. In 1974, we were lending at 4% pa to small borrowers like cobblers, shop owners. The maximum lending amount was probably Rs 5000. Here the banks got interest subsidy from Government at the rate of 6% so that our average cost of 10% was recovered. Following this the government started a scheme called Integrated Rural Development Programme (IRDP). Under this programme, every district was supposed to create a district credit plan.

This credit plan determined the various projects through which we could do expansion in agricultural initiatives or setting up MSMEs or any kind of commercial activities proposed by District Industry Centre.

Another initiative of IRDP was the Village Adoption Scheme. Every rural branch of the bank was supposed to adopt a village for overall development. In Hindi, it was called Sarvangin Vikas Yojana.

The Lead Bank Scheme, formation of NABARD and Regional Rural Banks, Sarvangin Vikas Yojana (Integrated Rural Development Scheme) formed the foundation of the rural banking in our country right since the 70s. Nationalisation brought in further benefits. But in

1980, the government realised that it is not enough. So Indian banking underwent the second trench of nationalisation.

And with this step, Reserve Bank of India started giving targets for priority sector lending. As per this initiative, 40% of our lending has to be in the priority sector, which comprises agriculture, MSMEs and services sector. This initiative is being followed even till today. But then the opportunity creation under this sector is the real challenge. For instance, let us look at agriculture.

Our landholding is so disaggregated that per individual, average landholding is not more than 2–3 acres. It may be even less. That being the reality, it is important to consider agriculture as an important economic activity for an individual. And that is why various initiatives in collective farming, collective irrigation, collective selling of the products through the agriculture produce marketing centre, followed by the Farmers Produce Organisation, many progressive things have happened over the years.

The latest being the Farmers' Produce Organisation; these are the entities which are available at the Panchayat level where they are supposed to really support rural growth.

This initiative has pioneered financial inclusion in a big way. All the economic machinery, all the government agencies, the lenders, when they get organised in one place and align on a thought, real growth can happen. That has been a great beginning. NABARD is an offshoot of that initiative; it was initially one of the verticals of the Reserve Bank of India but then NABARD was created as an independent Institution for agriculture and rural development. The lead district concept is a right fit to support NABARD efforts.

Financial Literacy

With all these initiatives, it was well understood in those times that simply having the infrastructure and policies is not enough unless there was awareness at a very basic level.

Especially when the Banks were asked to look at credit expansion, it was felt very necessary that there should be sufficient financial literacy in the villages, among the last mile customers. The challenge has been how do you really achieve that literacy. Therefore it was again a responsibility of each lead bank of the district to set up a Financial Literacy Centre in all districts.

Each district has an office of a lead district manager whose role is to supervise and drive the growth of that district. We had a representative of NABARD on my board in the Regional Rural Bank. That is how banks started opening rural branches in interiors, Financial Literacy Centres and creating awareness. Training centres for the RRBs were also created. In that manner, literacy and reach both could be achieved. Now these Financial Literacy Centres were initially set up at the District level but the banks in their prudence have gradually gone to the Tehsil level too. While the number of districts in the country could be 700 plus, the number of Financial Literacy Centres are much more. And I think that's very prudent because the very objective of the Financial Literacy Centre was not only to tell about the credit availability, but also how credit should be used, why the credit is required, what kind of productive activities can be taken up. These financial literacy centres have contributed a lot towards creating the awareness among rural citizens.

Thanks to these efforts, we have got more than 1000 financial literacy centres operating in the country with at least one in each district. As part of financial literacy, there needs to be a thrust on digital literacy at the field and branch level as well.

Financial and digital literacy at the grassroot level is important because when we look at technology solutions operationally, banks cannot enter into any transaction where they are not able to establish the identity of the customer or if there are any irregularities in their documentation. Issues for customers often arise from not only a lack of awareness of what financial products are available but also the formalities and documentation that will safeguard their savings and the bank as well. Awareness of technology and how to use it safely is another layer for literacy. Technology solutions are ensuring that customers are least inconvenienced. Other than cash, almost all transactions can be done digitally whether it is deposits or withdrawals in your account, or payments or KYC or a loan application. It is also important that financial literacy Centres operate in the vernacular languages. This helps people grasp key concepts easily. These days banks create various videos for the benefit of farmers, small businessmen and rural folk to make them understand what their products are all about and how customers can take advantages of these benefits. When we talk of literacy, it is not enough that we only open a financial literacy centre. We need to create enough tools to reach to every individual to make them understand all opportunities. Today this kind of content on 'finance subjects' is very popular on YouTube.

Literacy And Reach

These were the two buzzwords.

This is not an easy task, even today. There are almost 7 lakh villages out of which only around 40,000 villages have bank branches. Only 30% of our bank branches are in rural areas. Now how do you cater to each and every village?

If you do not create the reach, the whole effort has no meaning. The very first effort to create reach started in early 2006, when the concept of the Business Correspondent model was introduced in the country.

This was a very important Initiative, where private corporates had floated the corporate business correspondent units and recruited individuals from villages. We, as bankers, availed their services and deployed business correspondent agents to connect to the last mile and bring those people to the banking fold. Soon business correspondents became extended arms of the branch. Thus various business correspondent companies got institutionalized and they started giving the services as lead generators and as the first connects to the account. In those days, Madam Usha Thorat was the Deputy Governor and she was the driving force behind this activity.

These Business Correspondents were also given the responsibility of providing the various financial services particularly deposits and withdrawals of cash. The business service correspondents could provide mobile ATM services through hand-held devices that were all connected at the core banking level and all transactions were captured there. That was a positive beginning where banking services can be provided to each and every household, and banking transactions are properly captured and any fraudulent activity in the system is minimized.

Along with, the business correspondent model, the initiative of the self-help group started. What is a self-help group? It is a group initiative where 10–20 people join together and the women's self-help groups have been the most successful all over the country.

There are books and success stories written on the concept of self-help groups. There were many good small self-help groups developed in Chhatisgarh and there was a lady in Rajnandgaon, who was driving those self-help groups as a community. She won several awards as well. I was very fascinated. During my visit to that branch, I visited the rural area and tried to understand how these SHGs were working.

Observing this success, during my stint as Executive Director at the Punjab National Bank, I opened a dedicated branch for serving women customers and self-help groups in Rajnandgaon in Chhatisgarh in 2010. This was a branch dedicated to only self-help groups, where their savings accounts were maintained and where their borrower's accounts were maintained. We also did many activities to make them understand about savings, the importance of repayment, their liabilities and responsibilities. I found that there are two most important things which are required as a support to all small business players in the country.

One is the procurement of raw materials and second is the supply of their finished products. When you talk of procurement, as an individual, if I go to the market and want to procure something, I pay a higher cost. But take 10 SHGs, if their requirements are aggregated, if bulk purchases are made and procurement is done, I think the cost of procurement can be reduced significantly.

Ultimately for any business, the basic principle is cost optimization or minimization and profit maximization. Now how does the cost optimization happen? Collective procurement is big step. At the same time, there should be a good marketplace for the sale of your product. Let me give an example. Much before my experience in the Punjab National Bank, while I was in the Union Bank of India as a Zonal Manager for Mumbai Zone, the Mumbai Municipal Corporation also had the initiatives of creating self-help groups. And I remember having created a marketplace for all those producers to whom the Bank had lent the money. I was a banker to the Municipal Corporation also, and they wanted our branches to do this financing. So we created a marketplace by bringing the various buyers who happened to be our customers, the retailers, the wholesalers, the suppliers, the buyers – to participate in market and get a better price for their produce.

There were a couple of experiments we conducted in the PNB by engaging business correspondents. We had a common service centre in a branch in Bihar which was started to essentially service commoners for booking railway tickets, get birth or death certificate and other government services which commoners would like to do. We had designed this activity to identify entrepreneurs who could actually run and operate such service centres. We used to give loans to these entrepreneurs to float such service centres and then we also tied up with a private group to extend these activities in the rural areas, particularly in the districts where PNB was the lead bank. This experiment was a huge success in Bihar. Today such service centres are very common across the country. Besides I also had the opportunity to drive the State Level Bankers Committee for the states of Punjab and Haryana.

It was a great experience to drive the complete developmental activities of the State where the Banking industry is required to contribute. We needed to engage all the bankers, the complete community, the various State departments. That was a great learning for me as a second in command. Here I learned that all banking players in the State and the State Governments are taken on board to drive the programs which are bankable, and the activity is coordinated well, wonderful results can be ensured. It's not only political agenda which gets driven through banks, economic agendas can also be driven through SLBCs. Nothing is impossible if everyone is on the same page. I truly believe that the Dantwala committee which came out with the scheme of Lead Bank and State Level Banks back in 1975 has given a big boost to the growth of the banking sector and the rural economy.

I think similar efforts will have to be made by the bankers on an ongoing basis to bridge those gaps in banking facilities. In all districts, the lead bank should necessarily work on creating marketplaces for small producers and big buyers and ensure that a profitable deal takes place for all.

Pradhan Mantri Jandhan Yojana

Decades after this journey of inclusive growth commenced, the real magical transformation has been achieved in these initiatives with the launch of Pradhan Mantri Jandhan Yojana in 2014. We had a couple of schemes like MNREGA and other government subsidies being paid to the farmers. But this was all paid in cash and the government realised that there was lot of leakage in all this subsidy distribution. The primary responsibility was to arrest the leakage and ensure that the subsidy was reaching the right beneficiary. It is now digitisation that has really helped push the Pradhan Mantri Jandhan Yojana, where the objective is that every household should have one banking account and to have that banking account, your primary requirement is the KYC.

In earlier years, the main challenge was how to establish the credential of the account holder. We have Aadhar to thank for solving this challenge. Aadhaar is the biggest achievement of the country towards financial inclusion; it has given an identity to every rural person, where he or she lives and what he or she does and what his or her mobile number is. So it was Aadhar which authenticated all the banking accounts in the country and under PMJDY, the Banking Industry ensured that each account holder is linked to Aadhar for KYC compliance.

Direct Benefit Transfers

Taking cue from the Pradhan Mantri Jandhan Yojana, it was ensured that subsidies were routed through a direct benefit transfer scheme into the bank accounts rather than being paid in cash. Direct benefit transfer scheme has been a boon in plugging huge leakages which ran into thousand of crores. Today the subsidy is reaching the end beneficiary and the benefit has accrued to the last mile substantially.

But that is only one achievement in the area of banking. We now know that citizens in rural areas are not adequately insured. What happens if the family head dies? What happens if family property is damaged? That is how the Pradhan Mantri Suraksha Bima Yojana, Pradhan Mantri Jeevan Jyoti Yojna, and other Insurance schemes were launched with the help of the banking industry. Under these schemes, all the bank employees have been made to ensure that all account holders, particularly from downtrodden areas or lower strata of the society, are told about getting this insurance so that it helps them. For instance, if I have a driver working with me, I must ensure that he takes this policy. In today's world, for true financial inclusion to unfold, everybody needs to be covered under accidental insurance and life insurance.

Is Insurance for All?

Penetration has improved tremendously. But is it enough? No, it is not enough. Insurance penetration can be measured; when these schemes were introduced, the penetration was around 3% and even today it lags behind at 5%. According to the IRDAI, almost 87 percent of our population has no life insurance while 73 percent has no health insurance.

I say Insurance Penetration in India lags behind when you compare it with advanced countries with 52 percent coverage, we are still way behind. The Insurance Regulatory Authority has come out with the Insurance For All by 2047 scheme. We are only in 2024. The regulatory authority knows that to cover each and every individual eligible for insurance, it will take a couple of decades. It will also take a lot of sensitisation and lot of initiatives like Bima Vahak taken by the IRDAI to see that really the insurance reaches all.

The challenge with financial inclusion is that if there is any mishap with borrower, it ruins the very objective of the financial inclusion. For instance, if a family member has borrowed money and he is not insured. If such a person dies, then the family automatically becomes the debtor and has to serve the debt for their lifetime as well. That is how a lot of rural NPAs actually happen. It is mainly because they do not have access to insurance. Thus I very strongly feel that it is the responsibility of the banks, fintech companies, technology service providers that adequate digital literacy is created so that every individual should know that what are the services that he or she can use that will impact their lives.

Simplifying Lives

Where can banking play a role and simplify lives? For instance, when we look at migrant workers from Bihar, UP, West Bengal or Kerala, in metro cities like Mumbai or Delhi. How do they save their money? How do they remit money across to their families in rural areas? Initially they were serviced by business correspondents but it is time that they understood banking and banking operations. Today UPI allows you to transact from the phone itself. This simplifies operations and transactions in a big way.

I am on the Board of a company called Nearby Technologies, who are providing financial services through 4 lakh plus merchants in villages who have been given mobile ATMs, machines which can make the AEP (Aadhar Enabled Payment) transactions and all that. These merchants have been trained to be digitally and financially literate, to serve the end client. Perhaps through their 4 lakh merchants, they could be serving maybe more than 4 crore clients. These kind of services by various players should ensure that each and every individual of the country has access to the banking industry. Banks could take the support of various business correspondents who are operating in the rural areas. Fintechs, various NBFCs, housing finance companies, microfinance institutions should all create synergies between financial players to spread their reach to semi-urban areas and rural areas. Today the issue is that since the potential is low, companies need to be encouraged and incentivised to start operations in backward areas. So how do you make these services economically viable? The economic viability can be achieved through providing more and more technological services where by using those tools, the services are made available.

Present day bankers need to ensure that they can extend their services directly or through service providers and fintech companies or business correspondents in order to cater to the needs of the end customer in the rural areas.

Financial inclusion does not mean only access to financial services; it should also create opportunities for people in rural areas to increase their income.

As Economists or Bankers, we must realise that the poverty rate in our country is very high and the per capita income in rural areas is very low. If we aspire for inclusive growth, we must ensure that the average per capita income of rural people increases year on year so that we can move ahead toward becoming a developed economy.

So I believe it is very essential that we not only ensure that banking services reach them, but also that our services are availed by them for their economic growth. Bankers should take up the responsibility to evolve and work out what can really supplement, augment, support income growth in the rural areas. I believe this is the one thing that will definitely help us achieve Inclusive Growth.

As a banker I will constantly urge my colleagues to understand that inclusive growth means there is economic development of every household in the country. So that their per capita income increases substantially to match with the developed countries of the world.

Even today when we look at banking, with all the digitisation, we still deal with lot of paperwork, photocopies and so on. Till date there are still many Indians out of the fold of financial inclusion, how do we bring them into the banking fold?

Chapter 10

The Hand of Technology

Technology and paperwork are an intimidating factor for even educated people. So when we talk about financial inclusion how do we look at documentation and the tech challenges which are actually keeping people further away from accessing banking amenities. I think it has been addressed to a great extent by introducing the eKYC, video KYC whereby the bankers or the business correspondents are supposed to do the KYC digitally.

And when you are doing a digital KYC, if we have to authenticate something, there is a tool through which you give your thumb impression. It goes to the UIDAI repository and it gets verified. A small example is the life certificate we have to submit every year to avail our pension payments. Senior citizens have to physically go to the bank branch, wait in queue and then do this activity. Now banks have started sending links so that senior citizens can do their digital KYC while sitting in their own homes. To a great extent, initiatives have been taken so that paperwork is reduced substantially. But like I said, literacy is important – on the part of bankers, to be able to offer that technological convenience and, on the part of customers, to be able to avail that service.

Digital initiatives are the crucial steps for banks to offer differentiated customer service as well as financial inclusion.

Rural Borrowing

Another place where tech and digitisation will make a huge difference is Rural Borrowing. For instance, if we look at rural borrowers, a rural borrower may take a loan for a specific purpose and a banker will consider that application on the basis of his or her understanding of that business in that type of rural area. But he or she may not have sufficient knowledge or training to anticipate future problems in the ecosystem. Most NPAs in rural ecosystem happen because they are not aware of the larger issues that can impact the borrowing and have a contingency plan in place. For instance, what can be done if natural calamities happen. If I am an agriculturist with ready stocks, I need to dispose off the stocks in good time when the markets demand it. If suddenly markets get flooded with wheat or rice from other suppliers, you may not get a good price for your stock. This is when organisations like the Farmers' Produce Organisation come in handy.

These organisations are created to basically ensure that the farmers get all possible facilities to dispose of their produce at a proper price. Because when the farmer goes to the Mandi, it is a buyer's market and not a seller's market. But when the Farmers' Produce Organisation aggregates on behalf of all the farmers and then try to get the proper market price for the produce of their farmers, I think that is one concept which has picked up well to secure farmers' finance needs and the banks' lending.

Loan automation system

The other area where digitisation is making a marked difference is loan automation. As a banker, we look at reducing unproductive footfalls in our branches. Basically any transactions, like withdrawal of cash or getting a demand draft, that can be done outside the branch should be encouraged to be concluded on a digital platform. Now coming to the advances side, which you call assets, a banker gets the complete data digitally, on how the home loan is being serviced, what is the behaviour of my home loan accounts, how is the behaviour of the home loan accounts in different branches, in different geographies. Before digitisation and technology, there was a huge time lag between a customer approaching a bank and the loan getting processed, approved and disbursed. Today that situation has changed. Pre-approved loans are very much a norm.

Technology can to a large extent study customer behaviour for eligibility and push papers digitally from the branch to the administrative office where it is processed.

The biggest advantage of digitisation is always the standardization. Before digitisation was possible, all the information that was required for processing a loan proposal was prepared by the Branch Manager. The Branch Manager writes a story. This story is narrated in the way he understands. Another Branch Manager would narrate the same story based on his own perceptions. Therefore the loan sanctioning would be a subjective decision. But if standard tabulation has been done, if a standard set of questions have been answered, the decision of the sanction becomes more objective and less dependent on subjective perceptions. Similarly, once the documentation gets standardised, operational efficiency improves significantly.

I mentored Online PSB loans, in its earlier avatar was called Capitaworld. Even today, I continue mentoring it. Loan automation systems have helped reducing the time lag and processing time and improved the standardization of the process.

Loan automation has evolved to digital lending. There are a number of NBFCs and Banks who have introduced PSB 59 minutes. It is a platform where the applicant can push his application digitally and it gets processed also digitally. Before this application is delivered to the bank, it is processed from the credit bureau angle, income tax angle, and legal standpoint as well. After all this processing is done satisfactorily, it gets delivered to the Bank identified by the customer.

In Online PSB loans, the in-principle approval flows automatically in 59 minutes. These advantages have accrued over a period because of loan automation system. Another big advantage, which has evolved over a period, is NPA management. Loan automation and digitisation have led to significantly lower NPAs.

How sticky is your customer?

Another basic principle which bankers learnt because of technology is whether a customer treats their bank as a preferred bank. A customer may have a savings account with you. That is great. But does he or she have a car loan or an insurance policy? Or mutual funds? Has he or she approached you for a home loan or education loan? Unless you are ensuring that whatever are the basic needs of today's customers and whether your products are providing for these needs, you are not leveraging the true potential of your relationship with your customer. Now this is measured by a word called stickiness; improving stickiness helps you in growing your business and engaging your customer. But then the question is: Why should you be the preferred bank? If you are able to answer that question yourself and satisfy your customer, I am very sure you will be able to achieve a stickiness of 6 out of 10. So I would say that it is technology that has enabled this kind of customer-centricity. Customers also have become choosy. In earlier days, customers didn't have a choice but to go to the bank for every small task. Today they just have to go to the Internet and search websites for information on banking products, rates of interest. So while technology has improved customer's stickiness, it has also opened the vista of services of your competitors to your customer. This means customer is more aware and that is a good thing. To my mind, more competition leads to more efficiency.

Customer engagement in the age of digitisation

In earlier days, when a customer visited a branch, the front office was instructed to spot a good customer and request them to meet the Branch

Manager in the cabin or sit across the Accountant so that they could get personalised service. When you give time and attention to a customer, he or she will always seek to get service and will keep approaching you.

In today's age, documentation and the paperwork can be done online. Most transactions like, Fund Transfers, Fixed Deposits, Bank Statement, Cheque Book order can be done online. Now if customer is not visiting the branch at all, how does the bank engage with him or her? This is a big challenge of technology. In that case, customer engagement has to be developed differently. In the early days, bankers made best use of digitisation by using data to identify 100 top customers of the branch. Through technology, I can identify and reach out to this targetted group in a generic fashion. But as a Branch Manager, one needs to connect with these top 100 customers individually as well. A generic message on behalf of the Bank will not suffice. As a Branch Manager, I can personally message ten customers everyday and try to create rapport with them. In my experience, this works wonders in relationship building.

If it is a young couple, offer a home loan or car loan, something suitable to that customer. If it is a middle aged customer, offer something like an education loan or home extension loan etc. One must try to develop connect on a personalized basis.

These days it is possible to connect with groups of customers even in WhatsApp groups so that interaction is on an ongoing basis, with personalized messages. A group of like-minded or people of similar demography would be a good way to stay connected with customers and also attend to their business.

In today's age, technology can survey customer behaviour and spending patterns and identify those eligible for personal loans or credit cards or overdraft or other services. But the generic bombarding of messages declaring pre-approved loans, free credit cards is actually a disservice to banking. If you don't know the customer, how can you offer a loan or ensure repayment or that funds are being used for right purpose? What kind of customer will randomly take a loan he or she does not require? You may create visibility for your brand but that may not be the right way to win business.

The best method is to focus on certain target groups for certain products and try and convert them one by one.

Marketing does not mean only sending messages. Marketing means that ultimately your effort has to be converted into business opportunity. For this you do not need 500 accounts. You need to work on ten to 20 suitable accounts. When you approach 10 people, you will get to know that there are 5 possible prospects, out of which 3 may be medium and 2 could be hot prospects which will eventually convert into business. I then work on the 3 medium prospects and again try and convert them. Then I pick up another lot of ten customers.

In today's age, when there is footfall in the branch, there is a process they follow to identify a potential business opportunity and address it in the right manner to convert into business. Now a manager can invite few customers to have tea to develop an individual connect. I have been trying this since my early days as a Manager in Morva, a rural branch. Knowing that the Central Coalfields employees were my target customers, I would often go to their officer's club to play badminton and was an active member there. Those interactions helped me offer my bank's services to all the players there. Similarly, engaging with people during festivals, special occasions, sponsored events always worked wonders for bringing business to the branch.

Leveraging CSR events for Customer Engagement

In the banking sector, Corporate Social Responsibility (CSR) presents a prime opportunity to contribute positively to society while also enhancing the Bank's visibility and fostering growth, particularly among small businesses. By strategically leveraging CSR funds, banks can make a significant impact and build stronger connections with their communities.

One effective approach is to use CSR funds to create and support local platforms that directly benefit small businesses. For example, organizing regular local marketplaces or "melas" where small businesses can showcase and sell their products not only supports these businesses but also allows the bank to engage directly with the local business community. Such events provide a venue for businesses to gain visibility, while the bank's involvement demonstrates a commitment to fostering local economic growth.

When sponsoring cultural or musical events, banks can go beyond mere logo placement and active engagement. By setting up a stall at these events and having bank representatives present to interact with attendees, Banks can create a more meaningful connection with the community. For instance, participating in public events like Marathons with a team of employees not only enhances the bank's visibility but also fosters personal interactions with potential customers, reinforcing the bank's presence in a positive and engaging manner.

A more personalized approach, leveraging digitization, can be highly effective. Rather than adopting a broad, generic strategy, banks can use data analytics to identify specific customer segments and tailor CSR initiatives to meet their needs. This "sniper" approach ensures that CSR activities are not just a compliance exercise but are strategically aligned with the interests and needs of targeted groups, leading to more impactful outcomes.

Effective CSR is not just about financial contributions but also about active involvement. For instance, when donating resources like ambulances to hospitals, banks should engage directly with the beneficiaries—visiting the facility, interacting with medical staff, and understanding the impact of their contributions. This level of involvement ensures that CSR efforts are genuine and impactful, creating a stronger, more positive impression of the bank's commitment to societal well-being.

Additionally, involving employees and their families in CSR initiatives can amplify the impact of these activities. Senior management and their families can help identify underprivileged groups and the most effective ways to support them. This involvement not only increases the reach and effectiveness of CSR efforts but also fosters a deeper sense of personal commitment and connection to the bank's community outreach programs.

By integrating these strategies, banks can effectively use their CSR activities to enhance visibility, support small business growth, and engage meaningfully with the community. This approach not only fulfills mandatory CSR requirements but also contributes to long-term brand strength and customer loyalty, ensuring that CSR efforts are both impactful and aligned with the bank's broader strategic goals.

Chapter 11

Financial and Digital Inclusion Now and the Future

Digitisation is also bringing about a huge transformation in all the spheres of the banking and finance industry. It is evident in the volume and frequency of transactions we see all around. However the more significant advantage of digitisation is in the area of financial inclusion. India is a land of contrasts. There are many financial benefits and services which have still not percolated to the most backward areas of our country. It is important for bankers today to consider whether their products and services cover the complete gamut of audiences, right from your constituencies in rural areas to semi-urban and metro areas.

Typically a banker has to understand that the kind of services we can offer to rural customers are very different from those we can offer to urban customers. My initial experience of building business at the grassroot level at Morva Branch for the Union Bank and the Rewa Sidhi Gramin Bank and then in Bhopal, has sensitized me to the importance of Financial Inclusion for India. This experience has earned me many Industry. Awards and speaker opportunities but it has also further strengthened my conviction that the role of banking in our Society goes beyond just Deposit Mobilization and lending.

I have written earlier that banking is a lifeline of any economy and therefore no matter what strides we make in our economy or industry, true progress can be seen only when we meet the objectives of Financial Inclusion.

And it is important to get exposure to working in economically backward areas and understanding their priorities. Working in a rural area is not convenient for most modern bankers; families get inconvenienced, business development is tricky, living in rural areas is also not easy. But I would reiterate that it is extremely important for a banker to work and get exposure to rural customers and its challenges. The villages are the real India, what we know as Bharat, and experience in those areas will help a banker understand what impact his profession can make to the rural ecosystem.

Speeding Up Payment Systems

In the early days, there was only clearing of cheques. From that point, we moved to NEFT, RTGS and so on. That was the initial technology intervention for the remittances.

I was part of the Reserve Bank committee that came out with a white paper on payment systems in 2007. We ideated a lot on what kind of challenges existed and what technology interventions can be done to digitize payment systems in India. And it was efforts like these that went into the formation of the National Payment Corporation of India in 2009. Mr Narayan Murthy was the first Chairman of the board and I was on the board of NPCl, which is globally the best payment organization and their latest product UPI is now getting interfaced and integrated with the global payment systems in countries like Singapore and other European countries as well. NPCI spearheaded the transformation in payment systems and today probably India holds number one position in the payment system globally. This is because we handle huge volumes as well as small ticket sizes. In a population of 142 crores, if 70–80 crore form the user group, it is a big achievement for our country.

The technology and payment system has evolved in a great manner. If you go to a shop or a vegetable vendor, he will just give the QR code and you can make the payment right away. The mobile density in our country is very high. If the population of the country is 142 crore, there are more than 100 crore mobile phones available in our system. But whether everyone who owns a mobile phone also uses it for making and receiving payments, remains to be seen or monitored.

It is important to create awareness around payment systems and Banks, the Regulators and players like PayTM, G-Pay and PhonePe, need to play a dual role in this context: one is to create awareness of how these systems work and how to use the tech, and the other is to make everyone aware of how to make and receive payments safely and prevent frauds.

In today's world, there are several digital platforms like Online PSB Loans in the country, which are attempting to digitize all manual transactions. SWIFT India is also taking all efforts to ensure that all domestic Trade Finance transactions, and financial messaging related to Treasury Operations, Security Market Operations, get 100% digitized so that there is absolutely no paperwork involved. This reduces the risk of fraud, economizes on the processing time on both the sides. Operational efficiency not only economizes the time it takes to complete each transaction but also the costs incurred for the same.

When you work on a transaction for Treasury or Trade Finance or Security Markets manually, we need to deploy five people to follow all processes. When the same job is done with the help of technology, we do not need more than two people to process the transaction. Thus there is a lot of cost effectiveness when technology support is available. However all the banks today are working with Fintech vendors. We should also have to take into cognizance the concern of the Reserve Bank that these service providers are not regulated entities. Thus any kind of shortcoming or flaw on the part of the vendor could put the banks into a problem. That is how the Reserve Bank came up with the

Outsourcing Policy, where they have directed all the regulated entities on how to validate and ensure total compliance, including the CISA certification for Cyber Security. A lot of initiatives have been taken towards this aim. I believe that the implementation should also happen in the letter and spirit so that the benefit trickles down to the last mile. The whole objective of financial inclusion is this.

Unfortunately, India deals with a lot of traditional challenges when it comes to saving, managing or investing cash or money.

Resolving Traditional Challenges

You may have many well-intentioned schemes, but without mapping these schemes cannot trickle to the last mile beneficiaries. So what is most important is mapping of opportunities, then designing the schemes as required by the target clients and then executing the activity. There are some typical problems banking world experiences in Indian scenario:

Benefiting Smaller Businesses

For instance, we may encourage and disburse loans to smaller enterprises. But they won't be able to repay the loan and make profits if they cannot procure their raw material at good prices or even sell their products effectively for a good price. This means that supporting smaller enterprises with loans should also include provision of a fair marketplace. We tried this when I was in Punjab National Bank. For instance, in Muradabad in UP, every household is into some kind of arts and crafts, a lot of which is exported. But how much of those revenues benefit the artist himself? The profits go to the trader or middleman. So how do we ensure that the artisans benefit? Many successive governments, banks and financial institutions have taken certain efforts but there is still a long way to go to solve these systemic issues.

Creating Trust Towards Lenders

Another big issue is our traditional belief that borrowing is not good. Indians prefer not to take loans. As far as possible, people avoid it. They borrow from the community, relatives, friends, sometimes at higher rates of interest, but will not come to a bank to borrow. There's a tendency to not trust an external organization. That's why it is observed in some places in India, people do not put their savings in Banks either. That has somehow coloured the way we look at banking and borrowing. Therefore even today, banking has to take a lot of steps to create credibility or trust.

Even today, in the context of financial inclusion, the primary need is to replace the traditional moneylender.

Borrowing from friends and community comes at a huge cost. To give an example, there are vendors in the Mumbai wholesale vegetable markets who buy vegetables wholesale and sell them in their local neighborhood in retail. Most of these vegetable vendors buy vegetables worth Rs 1000 in the morning on credit and pay Rs 1100 to the lender that very evening. Now someone may say it is just a hundred rupees, how does it matter? But if you calculate the interest, the small vendor is actually paying Rs 100 as daily interest, which is 10% per day, whereas a bank would charge much much lesser. This is what was happening in rural areas as well and people are now slowly realizing that borrowing from a bank is better.

Recently, I had addressed the Bandhan Bank team on Ethical Banking and we had a discussion on the apprehension that people have when it comes to paying commission and interest. Today, we see Bandhan Bank which has transformed from a Microfinance Institution to become a mainstream Bank. It is because of this confidence and trust of customers and stakeholders which has fuelled its growth.

The only deterrent to banking has been this lack of knowledge and awareness. And the only solution to that is to create proper literacy, awareness and handholding. Banks also need to create trust in society.

Now to do this as well we need proper trained Advisors. When I was in the Indian Banks' Association, we looked carefully at the issue that Advisors in our industry were not recognised by any Regulatory Body. In developed markets like USA, there are registered Financial Advisors recognized by some regulators.

That's when the Association recommended to the Reserve Bank of India and they came out with guidelines and regulations for Advisors for MSME. In the long run, this credibility and transparency will help the cause of financial inclusion.

Simplifying The Lending Process

I have covered loan automation in the earlier chapters. When it was introduced, the customer was unable to apply for a loan digitally but the Branch or the Regional Office was able to push the application digitally to the sanctioning authority.

The system has helped in reducing the pain of the customer in submission of a multitude of documents one by one on demand. These days that problem has been addressed. Basically, the loan application will not go through unless you upload all the documents required. In 2016 Mr Jinand Shah, CEO of Capitaworld, approached me to help him on matters of technology in banking. He was also developing a solution for automating loan applications submission by borrowers. I shared several insights on the loan automation system platforms already in operation. But there was a huge gap on the processing front. Banks still needed help in processing loan proposals till it got delivered as approved or rejected by the Bank. Also there needed to be an element of clear objectivity to process the application.

In the traditional system, once the KYC and the verifications with the credit bureau checks, taxation authorities, income tax, GSTs were done, the loan proposal gets processed at the branch for an in-principle approval. This took a long time. We started working on the idea of how to automate these verification process.

We launched the beta version in 2018 with retail lending at the Union Bank of India itself. This experiment proved to be so successful that around 2020, SIDBI, along with four major banks, took over Capitaworld.

Now this banking solution is called Online PSB Loans (OPL) and the product is PSB 59 Minutes, which was launched by none other than the Honourable Prime Minister of the country, Mr. Narendra Modi. I believe that this product was successful because it is a result of a technology enabled solution through a banker's understanding of a customer's perspective. My inputs helped build an effective platform to cater to the needs of customers and I still enjoy being an Advisor to them.

Another important part technology is doing is in credit due diligence. Receiving the credit proposal is one part of the story but due diligence is crucial when you are dispensing the credit. Today there are a good number of companies who are able to do due diligence on corporates as well as MSMEs from a hundred-odd data points. Based on these data points, these companies are creating credit scores compiled from information which is submitted by various lendors to common Repositories.

The credit due diligence done by companies like Probe, Rubix and so on is touching on various data points, which include a customer's track record of GST payment, EPFO payment. If a company is not paying provident funds in good time, there could be labour unrest or if you are not paying the GST in time, there may be a liquidity constraint. All this affects a company's credit eligibility.

I have been a mentor for five years to Rubix Data Science, a data science company on credit due diligence, which is servicing not less than 100 corporates and 20 odd banks. Corporate entities use this software to check the credit records of suppliers, buyers and vendors. Besides due diligence, even monitoring and recovery has now been enabled by technology. I am also strategic consultant to SWIFT India which enables digitization of Trade Finance, Financial messaging in Securities Market in the country. Banks cannot anymore ignore the role tech plays in their growth. That's why every bank now has a Chief Technology Officer and also a Chief Digital Officer whose job it is to use the technology for digitisation.

Working Around The Socio-Cultural Constraints And Local Dynamics

I would like to share an incident from 1976. One young boy was helping me tour different villages around Morva Branch and scout business opportunities in neighbouring areas. He would sit on my bike and we would go around the area visiting people's houses. I remember he would take me to these big Brahmin households but would never enter these houses himself. I was received with great courtesy -- Bank Officers were a respected lot -- but the boy was never invited inside. I later realised that this was because he was from a lower caste. Caste is the biggest social challenge for our economy. No matter which rural area you visit, it is the same.

Do you know there is a caste background to even well-digging in some parts of the country? A banker will give approval to fund a farmer for the purpose of well-digging. But how do they identify exactly where the water source is closest to the surface on your farm? Today we have a machine to identify this spot scientifically and so the cost is much lower. But in the 70s, they had a strange method. They had a reverse catapult-shaped wood from the henna tree. A Brahmin man would hold the catapult high in the air and move around on the land. The catapult would bend at a particular spot and that would be the exact spot where the water was closest to the surface. I have done this myself although I have never understood how this work. It was being practised in those days in rural areas and this is how Branch Managers, when they lent a loan for well-digging, would follow as well. Because it is the spot which would cost the least to dig.

The local dynamics have not changed much. Now when we talk of benefits trickling down, can we ensure that all houses are benefiting equally with these measures?

I believe that some positive initiatives are required even from the Banker's side. If Self-Help Groups are so successful, why can't collective farming? And that is where I feel that some kind of initiative is required even from the Banker's side. Even if cropping is individual, at least, heavy equipment like tractors and water can be used commonly. These days, farmers in big centers are fully aware of the benefits of cooperative farming. They are getting into cash crops, fruits, exotic flowers, organic crops which add value to the produce. A banker can reach out to such groups and recommend options to farmers in their own language. That's why it is important for a banker to understand the socio-cultural context of the area and work with those local dynamics in mind.

Consolidating Resources For Small Borrowers

The other challenge for Indian banks in the interiors is that business owners or farmers have very little owned resources or land-holding. In such cases, even borrowing becomes very expensive. As a country, we have still not succeeded in collective farming. And here I would like you to read a chapter from a book called Jugad by Innovation, written by Navi Radjou, Jaideep Prabhu and Simone Ahuja. This book has a chapter about collective farming in Brazil. There is a success story of a person who moved from place to place and brought the farmers together and encouraged them to do collective farming. I am also privy to information on one of the farms in Zambia, because I was on the board of Indo-Zambia Bank. In Lusaka, we went to the rural area where I saw a farm of around 500 acres. It had a sprinkler with the arm length of 1 km. And that sprinkler of 1 km length would move around the expanse of the farm. But they could do this because of collective farming. You cannot get a loan for a tractor against a two acre land. It would be too much of a liability. If you want to have each acre of land well-irrigated, properly tilted with the tractor, and to experiment on different produce, you need to have the bare minimum, which is an economic piece of land of around twenty-five acres at least.

When I was a Branch Manager, I recommended to farmers with neighboring land to jointly borrow to finance diesel sets. Now even if you get the loan, a land of two acres will never give so much produce as to pay back my loan. So joint borrowing is the best. But they agree if the neighboring farmers agree to this only if they are from the same family or community. Now land parcels split with every generation. There is no reverse mechanism to put it back.

If 5–6 farmers pool in their land together, they could borrow jointly to get equipment for irrigation and farming. And the whole deal would be very economic for all of them. But this has not happened seamlessly in our country yet.

Collective farming, farm mechanization, irrigated land enhancement, community water management programmes are initiatives that really need to be pushed in our economy to bring best results. Banks could take this work of bringing together farmers to encourage collective farming or collective owned resources so that everyone can enjoy their benefits.

Contribution Of RRBs And Cooperative Banks To Financial Inclusion

This has been another traditional challenge for the industry. Regional Rural banks were created in 1975 and every State was mandated to have a couple of Regional Rural Banks. There were about 190 RRBs. The first step which NABARD took was consolidation and that led to tremendous improvement in cost efficiency. For instance, in a state like Madhya Pradesh or Maharashtra, there were 15-20 RRBs supporting all districts. Now every RRB will have back office costs, which get rationalized once consolidation happens. 190 RRBs have been reduced to 50 plus after consolidation. Today all RRBs are sort of an extended arm of Public Sector Banks, where the RRBs have branches where it is uneconomical for public sector banks. All RRBs are on core banking solutions, and so also totally technologically equipped and have a huge role to play.

Then we also have the Cooperative Banks. There are the District Cooperative banks, Urban Cooperative Banks and Scheduled Urban Cooperative banks. Now the Scheduled Cooperative banks are regulated by the Reserve Bank of India. But the district and urban cooperative banks, there are around 1200-1500 of them, are regulated by the Registrar of Cooperative Societies, of the respective States. As I see it, these banks are doing a lot of good work in their districts but there is still a need for transparency and ethical operations. This is because when any financial institution is led by a group of people, there can be a lot of vested interests when there are no strict regulations. Every third day, you read about some other cooperative bank getting its license canceled or something similar. Therefore these banks have to take it upon themselves to promote the cause of inclusive growth and maintain complete transparency and comply with the Rules and Regulations.

The only thing required is for Banks to walk beyond what they are expected to do at the Branch level. The banking community jointly, with help of Business Correspondents, Service Providers, NGOs, Commercial Organizations, move towards the nook and corners of their area of operations. Thus it is very essential that a proper synergy gets created in the process.

I would like to give an example here. I am associated with a very good NGO in Mumbai called Amhi Udyogini. This NGO is developing entrepreneurship skills in women entrepreneurs, providing them access to credit, suppliers of goods, and to the buyers as well.

Every year this NGO, as an incentive, takes its team of Udyoginis abroad to showcase and sell their products as an incentive.

Another example is FINO; it started as a Business Correspondent. As part of the Union Bank we had partnered with FINO on a few initiatives. It is now a Payments Bank. It was initially incorporated as a corporate business correspondent. And in 2007, the Union Bank had, with the help of their representatives, lent to 100 thela pullers, hawkers, vegetable vendors or sellers of other commodities. We took the help of FINO to identify these small hawkers, to monitor them and recover the credit. It was a big success. So financial inclusion has to be a collective effort. I would recommend that if banks are unable to do this outreach by themselves, they can engage with such organizations like FINO and drive these initiatives through.

Therefore it is not merely enough to lend money. Credit helps businesses but it is not effective on its own. It is more important to provide opportunities for work to expand. When there is a creation of opportunities for work, credit will then fuel growth and create a multiplier effect.

There is also a need to look beyond profit-making as a motive. Instead of thinking what's in it for me, the banking industry needs to think what's in it for all. Therefore financial inclusion needs to be seen as a contribution to Society.

The Pradhan Mantri Jandhan Yojana is finally making its impact. Banking industry is also taking efforts to ensure that every household has a banking account and the government is now able to ensure that the subsidies are getting credited to the right beneficiaries. Now once a beneficiary has a history of an account in a bank, this history helps identify those beneficiaries as potential borrowers for their credit needs as wellalso. Pradhan Mantri Fasal Bima Yojana, Pradhan Mantri Suraksha Bima Yojana, Atal Pension Yojana, all these schemes were conceived seeing the success of Pradhan Mantri Jandhan Yojana. Today we are making good headway with these kind of schemes.

When we talk of inclusive growth, I will say that the country can claim to have achieved it when our per capita income reaches the level of what developed countries have in terms of the percentage of GDP and the income level of the grassroot customers is brought above the poverty level.

So my message to the present day banker is that I always believed that I am not a lender, I am a partner in growth. If I am lending for a purpose, I must ensure that my borrower also grows so that he is able to pay me back. And thus I am a partner in the customer's business growth. If I am a partner in growth, I have to know about the subject. If I am a Rural Branch Manager, I must know about agriculture and local businesses.

Today we are in an age where even Paan Walas, Vegetable or Fruit Vendors also have a QR code and every housewife can pay by UPI. And these transactions are happening safely, smoothly. But as expected, has this reduced the usage of cash in our system? No, it has not reduced as much as expected. Cash in circulation as a percentage of GDP is still very high. But bankers need to promote digitisation as much as they can.

It would be too premature to discuss economic equality But we could decide what is the minimum economic level that every household should achieve. The government is playing its role and the banks must also contribute. Bankers can and have capacity to engage with the various agencies who are in the system to create not just financial literacy but also digital literacy. This way, technology will also be inclusive.

Chapter 12

Looking Back at the Future

As I said at the beginning of this book, when we look at our own lives as a bank account, we will always be conscious of what we are depositing into it. It is after all the effort, training, education, discipline and kindness we have put in that will compound over time.

A proof point of this was my appointment as Chief Executive to the Indian Banks' Association in the very week after my formal retirement as CMD of the Central Bank of India. This position was offered to me after a review of my work in the Management Committee of IBA. The IBA represents the entire banking sector which includes Public Sector, Private Sector, Cooperative Sector and Foreign Banks, and later the Small Finance banks and Payment banks. It has a sectoral committee for each sector and my role was to work for the benefit and growth of the banking industry, thus working for the larger cause of the society.

I would like to express my sincere thanks to all Chairman and Managing Committee members whose guidance and encouragement helped me to contribute to the larger cause of the stakeholders of the banking industry during my tenure from November 2013 to August 2016.

I was fortunate that I got an opportunity to serve our society with the launch of the Pradhan Mantri Jandhan Yojana in 2014. At the time, the IBA brought the entire banking sector together to deliberate and discuss how to make banking reach each and every household in the country.

Over a period of time, the Banking world leveraged the JAM trinity, that is Jan Dhan Yojana, Aadhaar card and Mobile banking.

It is a matter of pride for the banking industry that these steps in financial inclusion have saved thousands of crores of leakage. We have been able to ensure that Benefits and Subsidies have reached the right beneficiaries in their respective banking accounts directly.

We then focussed our efforts on Insurance and Pension too so that each and every Indian is covered so that every family is financially supported in the event of the loss of a family head. Today even a villager can contribute to the pension scheme. As one of the leaders of the IBA, I could think about the larger interests of the Society and the Industry. I was also able to think from the operational perspective of the banks: which geographies they operate in, what audience they cater to and what benefits they can deliver. I was able to understand how to optimize the deliveries of Private Sector as well Public Sector banks. This helped me interact and understand even more in detail how different banks operate and make decisions.

The other challenging aspect of my work with the IBA was in the area of non-performing assets. The NPAs had grown to a big number in 2013–2014. This was largely due to the heavy lending towards Infrastructure Projects to various Corporate sectors. The performance was not as per expectations. At the time, Mr Raghuram Rajan, the Governor of Reserve Bank of India, suggested to address the negative impact of NPAs due to a twin leverage, where on the one side the banking industry balance sheet is leveraged and on the other side, the Corporate balance sheets are leveraged. These rational initiatives helped us to address non-performing assets, how to restructure advances and how to revive them. As a result of these deliberations and initiatives, I am proud to say we have been able to lower the number of non-performing assets. We were also able to develop monitoring tools and a system with the help of which large number of situations to be considered as EWS (early warning signals); we were able to recommend SOPs to monitor the account regularly from day one. This led to the monitoring of SMAs (Specially Mentioned Account) right from day 1 of the default.

When I look at the banking sector evolution during the span of my career, I am very happy to see that the structure of our banking industry meets with the requirement of each and every constituent in the society. Public Sectors Banks have undergone consolidation from 28 Banks into 12 Banks and have got further strengthened leveraging Resources and optimising cost. Payment banks have started operations and you have an evolving sector called Small Finance banks which are catering to the requirements of the real small MSME groups. The cooperative sector has also geared up, be it the Urban Cooperative Banks or the District Cooperative Banks; they all have become tech-savvy and imbibed core banking solutions and are competing effectively with all other banks in the market. To supplement these efforts, there is in place a wonderful infrastructure of Non-Bank Finance companies, Micro-Finance institutions etc. In fact some of the small banks are the ones that have successfully converted from micro-finance institutions. I would say that many efforts towards inclusive growth are indeed successful. And I am happy that I have been a small contributor to this growth.

But going forward, given the country's requirement to meet the demands of a 142-crore strong population spread across more than 7 lakh villages, is this enough? No. Unfortunately the poverty level or the income gaps have still not been able to be bridged as much as required. While the economy is growing–we are the fifth largest economy globally–what is most important for the country and the banking sector is to ensure that the banking facilities, in terms of both servicing and financial support, are available to each and every household which helps them in improving their income generation and thus the financial status.

Focus On Agri-Business

As a banker who has spent a good amount of time in rural India in the 70s, my observation is that growth in rural areas has not been too satisfactory. Our banker colleagues need to focus on this aspect. We are an agri-based economy but we have not given required importance to improvisation of the productivity through land aggregation in some form or another. Secondly, although we have created the FPOs (Farmers Produce Organisation), there is no foolproof mechanism to ensure that farmers are being paid the right prices. We still observe intermediaries playing a major role in pricing. Bankers could play a role in ensuring farmers get complete facilities in warehousing and selling platforms to realize the proper price for their produce. Are we giving the right price to the farmers or still the intermediaries are having their majority share in the pricing? Bankers give crop loans; these loans are six-monthly and after every harvest, you are expected to adjust the previous crop loan. For this, one has to compulsorily sell the crops at whatever price they get. Instead of that if the crops are stored in the warehouses, raising the funds against warehouse receipts and selling at the right time, I believe proper price realization will happen. This will prevent the drainage at the level of intermediaries.

Catering To All

With Metro, Semi-Urban, Rural Branches of Banks, only 30–35% of the population is addressed. But what about the rest? Today if you are still doing the remittances through the orthodox methods, the UPI has come very handy. But UPI will have to tie up globally with all players so that the entire globe is one village rather than different countries.

But if you were to look at international transactions, so many migrants from Kerala, Punjab, Bihar have gone abroad. Are they in a position to send the money instantly to their family members in rural areas? Are those beneficiaries receiving the money instantly in their wallets or in their accounts? Can they use the money immediately?

Footfall In Bank Branches

The other issue of concern is the footfall in bank branches. The visits of tech-savvy millennial crowds have indeed reduced. But when you visit any branch in India, you still see crowds and queues.

You still observe customers frustrated with the paperwork and the waiting and the lack of customer service. The solution to this is that all services should be available at a customer's doorstep through technology. If not, the customer service should gear up to cater to customers when they visit the bank.

Can we erase the customer bank interaction completely and replace it with technology? It is neither possible nor advisable. Instead, I believe that the banker should encourage the customer to come and visit the branch once in a while. But that visit has to be an opportunity for relationship-building rather than a complaint forum. We are in the age of payment apps. One Branch is as good as another. Bankers need to assess what customers expect and how they can differentiate themselves from other banks.

Mobilization Of Resources

Another big challenge facing the Indian banks going forward is the mobilization of resources. The average investor or bank customer is aware of various investment opportunities. The mutual fund industry has grown phenomenally and so has the insurance industry. But when resources will get distributed to various investment opportunities, banks may not have that comfort of getting the low cost funds very easily or the growth of the deposit. This may ultimately also impact your capability to lend. Banking industry has always relied on deposits as a resource for lending. We have not really explored much on the market side to raise funds through the NCDs or other instruments which could also be used for onward lending. In the near future, bankers will have to consider this paradigm. Once the mobilization of resources is sorted, how does the banking sector compete with the other players in the market who are also in the lending business. There the real game is that of the price and efficiency.

Today's customer has no loyalty unfortunately and chooses products and services as per his convenience. Credit card usage has also increased. People are able to raise required funds just on their Credit Cards. They do not need to go to a bank and borrow. The credit card borrowing is further offered to be paid in monthly EMIs for customer convenience at a price. All banks will have to work very hard to ensure their prices are comparable and that can be achieved only through cost optimisation. Bankers have to start focusing on improving productivity.

Challenges With Technology And AI

When you talk of technology to reduce paperwork, we talk of Blockchain. Using Blockchain, one can move digital papers from one location to another. This technology can create a common warehouse where one party can push a paper on the Blockchain and the other party will have an access to verify those documents and the whole ecosystem can validate those documents. This validation is important so that digital paperwork gets the same cognizance as that of physical paperwork. To some extent, this technology is being used for trade finance transactions like letter of credit and bank guarantee.

In the coming years, artificial intelligence or machine learning will be used more and more to understand customer behavior and expectations based on various data points which are available. This analysis can help banks determine what they can offer to their customers. As informed earlier, I have been mentoring Online PSB Loans, which is an online banking platform for online loan submission of papers and which approves the loan in 59 minutes. By the time, application moves from the applicant to the banker, it gets processed in between. The application has its cross-checks with the credit bureaus and the KYC requirements.

I expect that the future of banking will be Account Aggregation, which is called Open Banking. These kinds of financial service platforms will use financial information of the customer with his or her consent and this will help service providers to recommend products to them. This will lead to customer attrition and movement from one bank to another bank which will prove to be a huge challenge going forward. Therefore what bankers need to focus on is to ensure that they cater to customers in such a way that they do not feel a need to move to another bank. However I strongly feel that Account Aggregrator platforms should be leveraged to extend credit to New To Credit Borrowers.

As AI is used more and more for customer service requirements, it can also impact the talent that banking attracts in the future. Banking has to now scout for talent that can use AI and machine learning and put in the right parameters that prompts to get the right data and solutions. Talent retention will go by what contributions he or she is making and whether the banking industry can honor and compensate his or her contributions. The challenge for the banking industry is to manage career journeys and compensation which will match the aspirations of the new age millennials. Banks should be able to convince their young talent that the organizational growth will ensure their personal growth.

The industry will need to constantly invest in reskilling and upskilling their teams to adapt to the changing dynamics in the banking sector. As a banker I can recommend that young executives work in all verticals which will give them a holistic perspective of how every department contributes to the overall operations of the bank. Today, a banking job is no longer the safe, easygoing job that it was in the 70s and 80s. Bankers are no longer only ledger keepers. Thankfully, even public sector banks have been permitted to hire at a lateral level for senior positions if the required talent is not available within the bank.

In today's times, some of the smaller private sector banks have also started offering employee stock options as well. Public sector banks also have to strategize on how to incentivise and recognise talent. It has to happen in an open or transparent process so as to retain their people.

Cybersecurity Is The Real Challenge

Of late, we hear that crimes have been committed with the involvement of the staff itself. This can be a deal breaker unless banks create awareness of the consequences of wrongdoings, formulate strong maker-checker systems and strong value systems created among the employees.

Today every bank has a Chief Information Security Officer who is constantly working on identifying vulnerabilities. The vulnerability assessment and penetration test, which is called VAPT, phishing simulation exercises and Disaster Recovery (DR) drills must be conducted on an ongoing basis. Cybersecurity is a matter of constant awareness creation; there is no total foolproof solution to completely avoid security risk. It is more about training and awareness creation and upgradation of technology to prevent cyber attacks. With all these measures, cybersecurity challenges can be addressed to some extent.

All in all, these are exciting times for bankers and I am proud that I have been a small contributor to this dynamic world. I often wonder what I would have done if I were not a banker. I probably would have been into academics. Teaching has been a passion for me since my youth. I have been a part of a study group since 9th standard. I was good at studies and my friends from this group would often come home to study mathematics with me. They would stay overnight, study late at night. My mother would make food for everyone. I still remain friends with this group.

Later on when I was studying Cost Accountancy, I was the oldest among the classmates and would often help them with their studies. That time too, we would study together as a group. These young classmates would come over home and we would study together. I would often solve their doubts. My wife would cook for all of us and make tea for us when we sat studying till late in the night. Of course, it has helped me in acquiring a professional qualification of a Cost Accountant. Today I am a Fellow of Cost and Management Accountancy.

This passion of learning and giving back has always been an inner calling. Even as a banker I have continued to pursue this trying to encourage my juniors to pursue further studies or to qualify for higher positions which I have continued.

This book is another effort in the same direction wherein I am trying to use my experience as a means to guide others in my profession. If it is one thing I have learnt as my father's son, it is that all personal growth has to lead to collective growth. I have tried to do this in a personal capacity as well as professional capacity as a banker. Banking can indeed facilitate people in fulfilling their aspirations. If I realized my dreams, it is because of my Seniors who led me in the right direction and thus I have to lend a hand to others around me to realize their dreams too.

Wise people recommend that we must dream big. But I never had a big dream. I only had small dreams and small goals. But I had confidence that I was always on the right path. I did well in studies and in extracurricular activities. I did the NCC and passed the A, B and C certificates. I was a cadet captain in the Navy while in college. I was given the SSB (Service Selection Board) interview opportunity for commission in the Navy without written examination. But I was confident even at that time that it was not my destiny. I always had a sort of confidence in my commitment and honesty that I would do well. And so I worked with small goals. When I was a Probationary Officer, I was already dreaming about becoming Manager and learning the skills required to be one. When I became Manager, I dreamt of becoming

Regional Manager and learnt how to get there. When I reached there, I looked at the top. I groomed myself to be a Managing Director.

All my endeavors in my profession have been to update myself. I am a voracious reader of the financial literature. All my career, I have carried the files home. My dining table always has heaps of files to read through. I sign a file only after I have studied a file thoroughly, made notings, done my analysis. This habit has helped me in every possible way.

I was indeed lucky to have Mentoring from my seniors in the Banking industry and also got full support from my colleagues and teammates.

Today when I look back to the youth I was, I never would have imagined that I could have come this far in my career. I could not have imagined that I would meet the President of India, Prime Minister of India, and even the Chief of World Bank in my life. I can't believe that I would ever lead a Bank, be part of so many exciting start-ups or travel the World meeting so many interesting people or even write this book. But I did.

If life is indeed like a Bank account, I suppose I must have made some good Karma deposits.

My sincere best wishes to dear Readers.